A Most Curious ⌐

Reaction to A Most Curious Detour

"After surviving his traumatic, challenging experiences
Stuart has gathered his thoughts then woven them
into a rich tapestry using every shade of colour.
Two things emerge for me having read this book:
That the human spirit is incredibly powerful and
that our stories are a key tool for transformation.
I recommend that you read this book, being thankful
that we do not need to pick up every piece of human
experience first hand to glean some crucial learning
from it."

"Tells his story from his own perspective, with great emotion and humour.
It is a story of hope that can be
an inspiration to others."

"A fascinating glimpse into the worlds inhabited by
a singular man who stubbornly refuses to let
the turbulence of life deflect him from his way of being."

"An important book.....well written."

"A book that could help many people."

(Because some professionals don't wish to be named as it might
compromise their work, I have left the quotes anonymous.
However, I can assure you that they were made!)

Contents

Foreword

Stuart Hepburn was born in Edinburgh, Scotland, in 1952.

He graduated from Edinburgh University in psychology and sociology having arrived to study business and accounting. Towards the end of his career he worked as a self employed business consultant with several large organisations, such as NEC (Europe,) British Aerospace, and British Nuclear Fuels.

From radically inclined youth and yogic monk, (though he would reluctantly describe himself as such), Stuart tread his own path, latterly enjoying what would be described in Western terms as a successful and rewarding life running his own business.

Imagine everyone's surprise then when in March 2005 he suffered an extensive stroke which initially left him completely paralysed, with no speech and at times near bereft of life.

In typical fashion he refused to succumb. Emerging from, the depths of his condition, he applied his life's learning to his situation and began to effect a slow, laborious recovery.

Stuart continues to apply the deliberate burn of his willpower to defy early predictions about his future.

A stage production of this book will appear in the 2012 Edinburgh Festival Fringe and at other venues.

Stuart's second volume, "Some Really useful Hints for a Successful Life," can be obtained from amazon.co.uk

A Most Curious Detour

A

Most

Curious

Detour

Stuart Hepburn

ISBN 9871-4457-8896-8

Dedicated

To the memory of

Jean Dominique Bauby
Author of "The Diving bell and the Butterfly"
Who showed that there is a mainstream audience out there prepared to listen to this sort
of
experience

And

to
Brian Keenan
Who, inadvertently gave me the key
to escape from my own nightmare

And finally

to
The Organ Grinder
Without whose rhythms I would
most certainly be a very static monkey

Acknowledgements

This book is dedicated, in addition, to all those who made it happen.

To Marnie Roadburg for her painstaking efforts in relentlessly reading and re-reading this text, long after it seemed to lose it's meaning, and for her dedicated enthusiasm in trying to cull my commas, unsuccessfully, as I think you'll discover!

And also to Pamela, who'll be thrilled to see her name printed in one of her beloved books, books that she seems to wade through endlessly. Although, by the end of this book I was mercifully less dependent on her than at the point where the story starts (I daresay she's happy too) it is a journey that I would have been unable to make without her constant love and support.

In addition, there was the invaluable assistance of all the staff, without exception, at my day care centre. This includes those who work behind the scenes. Particular mention should probably go to Linda Gibson, my Occupational Therapist there, who works tirelessly to convince me that Occupational Therapy is a hallowed profession, and to Alasdair Kane, my key-worker, who just works tirelessly. And then there's Alex Lodge, my art tutor, who has almost convinced me that there is some merit in my artwork! She was also the catalyst for this book.

Then there was Vikki, who helped me complete my artwork and who helped add a little zing to it.

And then there are all my carers, who put up with a lot for a very modest reward!

There is also my Mother to mention here. Over the years, but perhaps more so latterly, she has proved an excellent practice ground for any lofty spiritual principles.

And finally, there were two of my ex-students who took the time to visit me during the period of my rehabilitation and whom we probably all expected to be around long after me. As it turned out, disease was to come calling, unexpectedly, at their respective doors. I'm talking here about Iain Fraser and Celtic Queen, Eileen Bowry.

Introduction

I spent most of my working life coaching executives, encouraging them, not just to dwell in the territory of complaining of how bad things had become, or reflecting on how things had been in some ideal- ised past. I would encourage them, instead, to step into that head- space where they, and ultimately, they alone, had the opportunity to concentrate on how they wanted it to be in the future, and on how they were going to act in order to make it how they wanted it to be. Though, it would be nice for them to have some company for the jour- ney.

My entire career had been centred around the issue of equipping people for the challenges that lay ahead. It was against this background that I was reluctant to write this book. I thought it might lead you into sadness or sympathy, neither of which I regard as a desirable outcome.

It was only when a day centre worker said that it might help to foster greater understanding of my condition and help any people in a similar situation that I agreed to delve into my own experience. Experience of, first, having a brain stem stroke or series of strokes, and then, of spending the subsequent two years in three separate hospitals.

So, in this story I make public that which had remained very private hitherto. This material may be new to you, but its part of the fabric of my experience and has lain here for several years. So it's not new to me.

Strangely, it is me, perhaps, who has drawn the greatest benefit from setting this story down on paper.

At this book's outset, I can see now that I had the consciousness of an underground reporter. My identity was still that of an able-bodied person, reporting back to an able-bodied world about life as a disabled person. But by the time I reached the end of this book, I was reconciled to the fact that I no longer belonged to that able-bodied world. I had grown more comfortable (though perhaps, yet, not totally,) with my new life in this strange landscape that we call "disability."

At the outset, there was probably also an unconscious desire to gain the approval of the peers I left behind in the able-bodied world. But, as this story has unwound, I have come to the realisation that my mental well-being is far too important to leave in hands of people inhabiting a parallel universe, even though I once lived there too. I have, instead, found a much more reliable source of emotional support, but more of that later.

One other area I have struggled with, since the beginning of this book, is an area that I used to refer to, during my career, as "perceptual positions," the ability to "see yourself as others see you." In the business world, I had used this skill as the basis of getting past conflicts, and for effective negotiating. But now, I found it almost impossible to step into the shoes of another person and predict accurately what others might see when they looked at me. I just can't be sure of how much of, what I regard as the "real me," is still there to be seen on the outside. Certainly, there is a preponderance of people who think that raised voices and very deliberate pronunciation is the most effective route to take.

And at the beginning of this book, it was probably still important to me to correct any false impressions. But, by the end, I got that people see very different things when they look at me, and then attribute to my actions some widely different motivations. And, while this used to be a major source of frustration, I am now content for people to reach whatever conclusions they like, knowing that these conclusions reveal more about their lives, than they do about mine.

I remember, from my days browsing through the non-fiction departments, how non-fiction seemed to fall primarily into two camps. There were those who had achieved great things, and had then chosen to write about them. And then there were those ordinary people, who had endured remarkable "journeys," and, as a result, who had found themselves with something unusual to share with the world at large. I, probably, would have preferred to fall into the former category. But circumstances have conspired to put me into the latter category, so I guess I could just be grateful to be in the department at all!

By reading these chapters you enter into my world even if you, unlike me, are free to step out of it at will. It is now you who's being invited to make the step over from that other place.

A friend of mine recently asked if it was hard having a colourful future snatched away, and she asked how I coped with the sadness of this loss when I thought about it. The answer that I gave is that I don't think about it. It would probably drive me mad if I went down that alley. I focus, instead, on the next hurdle to be crossed. And, there is nearly always at least one on the horizon!

Visitors don't come by now very often. And for that reason, it is a great honour for me to have you over. As they say here in Edinburgh, "You'll have had your tea?"

This story becomes a little hairy at times, (by most people's standards).However, it is important to me that you see in it the triumph of the human spirit, as well as the adversity. It is not meant as yet another reason to be frightened. There's more than enough already!

A few years ago, I had the privilege of interviewing Brian Keenan, the man who had been caught up in the Beirut hostage crisis. I remember being very touched when he talked about his, almost, daily beatings.

He talked of realising, as he was being beaten, that he was the one who had the power. He could choose to forgive his captors, even if they didn't possess the flexibility to be anything other than the loutish bullies they had become. From him, I learned that, it is not the hand that you are dealt that defines you, but your response to the hand you are dealt.

I readily admit that there are probably moments during the unfolding of this story when I have gone for the sympathy vote. The sheer scale of what I was experiencing led me, from time to time, into "victim mode."

"When the going gets tough, the tough get going!" Well, it's got mighty tough, thank you!

I am told that I am quite critical of aspects of the NHS and of some specific professions in this book. I have deliberately not toned down that criticism because I have tried to portray my experience as honestly as possible and, at the time, I wasn't always feeling totally positive about how things were. Of course, looking back on it now, I can appreciate the problems of stretched resources and so on. But in this book you will find an honest account of my sometimes less than appreciative experience!

I have set things down in this book as I experienced them. This means that you, like me, will have to work out what's real, and what's imagined. However, to improve your comprehension of a fairly muddled story, I have set down the text in two formats. What I now consider to be "real experience" is set down in normal typeface. What I currently

accept as being "imagined," even though it was very "real" at the time, is set down in italics.

Though, who knows, some of it could be true? And, I am reliably informed, by fellow travellers who were present at the time, and who saw events unfold, that much of what is depicted in normal typeface, belongs in italics. But, since this story represents my own perceptions of what I experienced, I have stuck to my version of events, even when this conflicts with how others remember these same events.

Chapter 1 A Most Curious Detour

Believe it or not, I was once like you (assuming you were, at least once upon a time, reasonably healthy and moderately wealthy). I was travelling, nonchalantly, down the highway of life and just watching the territory unfurl before me. There was the awareness that Lady Luck was in the rear and that she had, so far, kept me out of any major scrapes.

It was nothing special, just a pretty contented life. My life had been a contemplative one, stretching back over thirty years (the contemplation, not me. I'd passed my fifty-second birthday when this story begins!)

And there had been comparatively little in the way of self-indulgence. I had studied Taoism. I had even dabbled in a little Tai Chi and a little Kung Fu.

I like to think that I had lived my life in a way that was harmonious with the world around me and in a manner that had even inspired others to do likewise. Balance and harmony had become the guiding principles of my life even though I was often found wanting in terms of both, as my wife would be pleased to testify.

Old age lay just beyond the horizon, and as it was still some distance away, it was not yet clear what mysteries lay in store there. Despite the fact that I was already fairly well travelled there were still corners of the world, out there, to be explored.

And then, out of nowhere, came the juggernaut. Straight into me, shunting me onto a new and very odd minor road, which meandered through some very strange countryside. I noticed that Lady Luck had made a hasty exit. The Grim Reaper, his scythe dangling worryingly,

behind my neck, now took her vacant seat. My life suddenly took a whole new direction.

A Most Curious Detour

A most curious detour had begun......

Chapter 2 The Trauma

It was a March afternoon, which meant that it was quite cold outside, and the daylight began to dwindle about half past three. I remember doing star-jumps at lunchtime, partly as a way of keeping warm and partly as a way to overcome the stresses of the morning. I was getting ready for my next "gig," a training course that I had been running in several modules, over several months. I was a self-employed business consultant and trainer, with several major clients on my books. Business had been steady, but not spectacular, and I was actively pursuing other business options, which would give me an even better return.

These were nothing more than cash-cows, regular sources of income. I was earning about half of what I'd been earning, a few years earlier, in the south of England. It was a fact that I put it down, rightly or wrongly, to the emphasis we often place in Scotland, on competing on the basis of the cheapness of our inputs and of keeping costs (including training costs) down. Don't get me wrong. I still think the Scots are God's chosen people. (In fact, I know we are. I just don't want to upset our English neighbours who, periodically, like to operate under the illusion that they are (especially in soccer World Cup years!) But, the parable of plucking out eyes until everyone in the land is blind, seems appropriate here. Maybe, we are ready now, in Scotland, for a bit more competition on the basis of the quality, of what comes out at the other end, rather than just focussing on how cheaply we can organize our inputs.

I suppose, I felt that my present line of work was not providing me with the return I aspired to. There seemed to be a lot of input, for a relatively modest return, although I enjoyed the work immensely. I had also reached that point in my life where, instead of making other people's dreams come to fruition, I wanted the experience of making my own dreams come true. I had come to the point where, I wanted to feel, for a while, what it was like to step away from being kingmaker, in order to experience what it was like being a king. This was probably a mistake, as kingmakers rarely make good kings! The competencies are quite different. With this end in mind, however, I had started mapping out a few projects, to be developed in any down time that came my way.

It was about 4p.m. and so it was just beginning to get dark outside. And it was a Friday, so the weekend promised a bit of rest. I was on my own, as my wife, Pam, had recently taken up a post, as Head teacher, at a primary school in Aberdeenshire, about four hours away by car. One distinct possibility was that I would close my business, and move to Aberdeenshire, although there were several options under discussion. One was, me going to live in Aberdeenshire, and taking a local job. Another was Pam returning south. But, that didn't seem likely, as she was heavily committed to her job, and to the local community. And finally, there was the possibility of us both acknowledging that our interests kept us apart, and that, maybe, it was time to formalise the situation. This tangle was still unresolved, on that cold afternoon in March.

I was in the room in our house that we referred to as "the office" Coincidentally, I was surfing the net in order to source a model of the brain, to be used as a prop, during the delivery of my next training module, which included, oddly, a piece on the functions of the brain. In addition, I was listening once again, on-line, to what I considered to be, some very interesting lectures on Neurosurgery, which were part of the Reith lecture series, recorded in 2003. In them, Professor Ramchander talks about some of the tricks that the brain can get up to in the case of some brain-damaged patients. I had, pretty well, made the effective use of the brain, or more particularly, the effective use of the power of the mind, the basis of my approach within client organisations.

Then, quite painlessly, I noticed that my legs were not working. My immediate thought was "I hope my legs are back to normal for next weekend, because I have a seminar to deliver." I managed to drag myself into the hall, and then having proved that I could still get about, decided that it would be a good idea to call for help. I don't remember mentioning double vision, but from that moment on, I was never able to see a single image again. It wasn't particularly dramatic, and, in my case at least, there was no pain involved. I didn't even know what a stroke was at the time. So I was not too bothered about my predicament, apart from the timing. It wasn't leaving much time for the doctors to fix me, and get me back up and running!

At this point, I assumed that my future still lay further down the highway, which had been stretching ahead of me, and which disappeared into the distance. I dragged myself to the front door, to await the ambulance that I had summoned. Although my speech was a little slurred, it was still in working order. A few minutes later, the ambulance arrived, and I was fit enough to sit up and answer the door. Two ambulance men came into my house. I remember answering a series of questions, but I don't remember what they were.

As I was carried out, into the busy Friday rush hour traffic, I remember a curious sense of shyness descend upon me. Never one to excel in public settings, little did I know of the sequence of ordeals that lay ahead of me, in the months and years ahead! It was getting quite dark now, but the presence of an ambulance, half parked across the pavement in front of my home, seemed to have attracted a small knot of on-lookers. For a moment, I swapped roles, becoming an on-looker myself, watching the drama, as this body was carried out to the ambulance.

Once I was safely ensconced in the ambulance, I realised that it was a Friday, and that the traffic, on the City of Edinburgh by-pass, which we would have to take in order to arrive at the hospital, would be at its worst. I remember thinking that this state that I was in was no

fun, and that, the sooner we got into the hospital, the sooner the doctors would be able to restore matters, to normal service. The ambulance seemed to make good headway. There were no sirens blaring,
but the ambulance hardly seemed to stop. Perhaps they were using
the hard shoulder.

I remember throwing up in the ambulance. I was reminded of an earlier occasion, when I had had a mid-ear infection, and when, effectively,
the whole world had seemed to spin. Perhaps this was a recurrence.
My first concern about the throwing up incident was for the poor ambulance man, whose ambulance must have become quite unpleasant.
But, there was also some emotional relief. For, if the ambulance man
had thought I was just making up my story about my legs not working,
then here, at last, was the tangible truth that something was not
right! I spent the remainder of the journey with a small up-turned
hat, made from paper pulp, balanced on my lap in case there was a repeat performance! But thankfully there was not.

Curiously, I remember pleasantries being exchanged with other ambulance staff, and with the hospital porters with whom my two ambulance men seemed to be on good terms. It seemed a bit odd to hear
such pleasantries exchanged during what, for me, had become such a
traumatic experience. It all seemed a bit incongruous, somehow, to be
exchanging pleasantries at a time like this. And then it clicked; this
was a routine Friday afternoon, and for these people, the world was
still going round. There was no doubting that the world had stopped
for me. Although, I certainly never suspected for a moment that I
was about to get off for a two-year period. If you had asked me be-
forehand if I could have survived for two years in the hospital system,
deprived of my beloved independence, then I would have had to say no.

I was wheeled into a receiving area, and put on a trolley in one of the
curtained bays. After a short while, a doctor came to listen to my
story.

And then, there followed a period when nothing seemed to happen. I think that there were at least two other medical visits, that night, including a nurse who had managed to find a sandwich for me. I remember puzzling over my inability to focus on a single image. I quickly learned that both eyes worked okay independently, apart from some black dots that streaked across my retina, giving the impression that there were black mice scurrying in all directions. It was a highly unnerving situation! The continual movement of the black dots gave me the sensation of being in a very busy room, and no amount of "internal dialogue" about looking rationally at the dots, would change that.

The lights dimmed suddenly, and we were given the clear message that the area was closed to business. The occasional inebriated patient was wheeled past, oblivious to the trauma that had touched my life that day.

And a knot of about ten nurses, male and female, gathered round the nurses' station, further up the corridor. They were discussing movies in, what sounded like, their normal voices. I, certainly, had no difficulty in following their discussion from a distance of twenty yards. Every so often, there would be an explosion of laughter, and I was reminded of my own youth club days, during which, the theme under discussion served as a thinly disguised form of flirtation.

As I recall it, I slept pretty well until the cleaners clattered round the area, emptying the rubbish bins. This must have been around 6 a.m. Then the staff started gearing up for breakfast, although I have no memory of receiving any. It was late morning before I was wheeled into, what looked like, an operational area. I remember being struck by how young the doctors were, their late twenties, I would guess. One young doctor approached me and said "Mr Hepburn, I'm Dr so and so, we think you've had a mild stroke." This didn't mean much to me, since I didn't know what a stroke was, and nor had I ever met anyone with this condition. So there was no emotional reaction to this development.

I was mildly pleased that they had a name for this "disease" and was fully expecting that they would give me the appropriate medicine and let me go back to the preparation that I was doing for the next weekend's training course. The model of healing that I carried with me was a kind of Disneyesque belief that things had a happy ending.

At a spiritual of level, I also believed that we co-create our reality. Yet, this latest development didn't seem to fit that model, in so far as; I certainly, didn't see this ball coming. There was no chance of a meaningful meditation, amidst this lot! For the first in my life I felt very spiritually "exposed". It would have been much easier to have a spiritual "intermediary" stepping in at this point although, that would have been contrary to my beliefs about spirituality versus organised religions. It had always been a core belief of mine that an "intermediary" wasn't necessary to a meditative life-style. And that the proliferation of organised religions was due to the fact that most people had surrendered their right to a direct experience in favour of a relationship conducted through an intermediary.

I realise that this might challenge the beliefs of many of my readers, so it is important to me to make clear that I am not setting out here to be offensive or disrespectful of somebody else's belief. I merely want to be clear about what I hold to be true. And, in the fullness of time, I suppose one of us may be proved right, even if you are very cynical about this entire area of human experience!

I was later to discover that the part of my brain, that I had used to meditate throughout my adult life, was damaged during my strokes. I was left, like a radio set, without a tuning button. I could go through the motions of meditation, but I had to use my memory of previous meditations if I wanted to experience anything. It was a bit like driving through life without a sat-nav, for the first time in many years. It felt very strange, after a lifetime of having things mapped out for me. In the absence of any simple explanation for this sudden change in my fortunes, I concluded, at the time, that the most constructive interpretation that I could put on events was as follows: that, at an unconscious level, I must have chosen this strange detour in order to demonstrate how it was possible to recover, even from a serious condition.

I had spent my adult life in the role of "leader." So, I could only make sense of this current chapter as yet another setting in which I was destined to devise an escape route, and, when the time was right, to lead some kind of "break out." I was trained not to waste time and energy by asking, "Why had this happened?" I knew that the list of "probable causes" was endless and that years could be spent on the psychiatric couch in an attempt to find the new "best fit" solution. Nevertheless, there was a nagging question in my mind about the extent to which I was responsible for manifesting this dreadful condition.

My next recollection is of being in a large space, with curtained bays all around the edge. I tried to say something to the nurse but was oddly unable to get the words out. I remember crying like a baby, partly through fear, partly through frustration. First my legs had let me down, and now my voice was doing the same. This was a truly hellish state to be in! It certainly didn't occur to me that I had spoken my last words! A little medicine from the doctors, now that they knew what was wrong with me, and I would be fine. But meanwhile, this voice thing was a pain in the backside! And, what about this crying?...........

Even now, I was aware that there were doctors and nurses looking anxiously across at me. In the absence of my voice, I reasoned that I still had my ability to write. The problem was that, for some reason, the nurses seemed to ignore my request for a pen no matter how many times I signalled. I was getting frustrated now! They asked me what my Mother's telephone number was. I had no idea. It was programmed into my mobile so I hadn't bothered remembering it. I tried to write it down from the Contacts List, in my mobile, which was in a bag that the ambulance men had, thoughtfully, put together.

Looking back on the whole situation now, it resembles a Brendan Behan play that I had come across many years previously. As I remember it, there was a tramp character cycling along a towing path which, in turn, ran alongside a canal. The bicycle wheel buckled so he threw his bike into the canal, reassuring himself that he could still walk. After a few miles further on foot, his shoe leather gave way and he found himself face down in a puddle. "Not to worry," he said to himself, (only knowing Brendan Behan's books, it would probably be more colourful language!) "I can still crawl!"

I was to learn, much later, that the nursing staff had worked their way through the phone book entries for "Hepburn," asking all and sundry, "Do you know a Stuart Hepburn?" until, eventually, they came to my Mother's number. When they made contact with my Mother, they were able to ascertain that my wife was a primary Head teacher in Aberdeenshire. So, they were able to trace her through the council HQ in Aberdeen.

Even then, I realised how cut off from the world I had become. And there was a nauseous realisation of just what it meant to be so close to people, yet, at the same time, to be so remote from them, and indeed, from the ability to summon help, let alone from the ability to explain just exactly what the problem was.

Over the years, I suppose I had built up quite a comprehensive "mental map," with lots of subtle distinctions, together with the verbal fluency to communicate them to the relevant health professional. So, under normal circumstances, I was able to get my needs met with little difficulty. The sudden loss of this facility, which I had taken very much for granted, left me feeling very vulnerable indeed. The loss of human contact was probably felt most keenly at the moment normal communication ended.

Thereafter, it was a question of coming to terms with my new identity, even if that process was to take years, rather than months. Subtle social signals had become the mainstay of my business life, and yet here I was, in a hellish scenario, where it seemed that I had lost the capacity to communicate even the most basic of my needs to those around me.

With hindsight, this tale does seem a little bit melodramatic. But, I can assure you; it was pretty terrifying to be at the centre of this little lot, at the time! This sequence of bodily malfunctions defied logic and was totally outside the parameters of my entire lifetime experience.

Fortunately, if there was any thing fortunate in this story, Pam was just about to embark on a break so it was not difficult for her to tear herself away from Aberdeenshire. There was still a decision to be made by her, as to whether this was an opportunity to walk away, and say, "Not my problem! " I'm pleased to say that, this was never an issue, and Pam was destined to be "my rock" in the weeks and months and for that matter, years ahead. During all that time, she was my "touchstone" on reality.

She became much more important to me than a wife; she was my very fragile grasp on sanity helping me to separate out what was real in my experience from that which was simply imagined. Even then, I was convinced that were some issues, about which, she did not really grasp the full implications. But, she was not in a position to grasp these issues in the way that I was. I reasoned that her lack of belief in some areas of my "experience" stemmed solely from her not being around when things were actually happening.

It is hard to exaggerate how important to me she was, at that time. And, on the one occasion that she arrived a few minutes late, I convinced myself that she wasn't coming and worked myself into a bout of hysteria, with lots of tears. She walked into my room and couldn't understand why her absence had been such a big deal, especially since she came to visit me every day, (at a car parking cost of £1000 over a three month period, I was to discover later!) But, she was not only my lifeline to reality. She connected with a part of me that the nursing staff had no idea was there. And she became my advocate, intervening in processes that she knew to be alien to me and correcting aspects of my care that were being overlooked.

It is difficult to exaggerate the need for a vocal advocate at a time of complete vulnerability. True, she didn't always get it right, sometimes reflecting her own priorities rather than mine! And her interventions weren't always as subtle as I would have liked. But, she was always in my corner, and challenging practices that she thought needed to be challenged. Above all, she treated me with the respect of someone who has been round the block a few times, in contrast to the nurses who tended to shout and treat me like a bit of an old imbecile.

A short time after my voice packed up I was taken for a CT scan (whatever that is)!

The scanner looked conventional from the outside. A tubular thing, into which I was slid on a mobile "bench" like a drawer. But, it was only when I got inside that I realised that this one tube was in fact the centre of a whole warren of other tubes, leading off on both sides. Indeed, there was an entire network of interconnected tubes that had been completely invisible from the outside.

I was surprised that no one had mentioned this to me. As I was about to learn, there were a great many of my experiences, which the NHS didn't seem to want to talk about!
After the scanner adventure, I was wheeled to the ward that comprised one of the three assessment units. A corner spot was given over to my use and my mother, brother-in-law, and niece, were seated round my bed.

As I remember it, we were engaged in the usual kind of hospital chat, about visiting times etc when there came the sound of flowing water as though there was a pressurised hose nearby. To my horror, I realised that my bladder had just emptied in the bed in which I was propped up.

This was turning into my worst nightmare! First my legs, then my voice, and my ability to write, and now my bladder! And, I was particularly upset at the thought that the nursing staff might confuse me with one of the Friday night boozers. Or even worse, that I had done this out of laziness!

Whatever the case, I was now totally unnerved by the series of events that had been unfolding. All of this came on top of the double vision that I was still getting to grips with! This was now reminiscent of my worst hangovers. I was not a happy bunny! Though, I'd have preferred not to announce it to the world, by bawling my head off. This was something that I felt strangely compelled to do! I found out about emotional lability much later. This occurs when the brain-injured
person loses control of their emotions. Consequently, the bawling just "happened" and I was as surprised about it as everyone else.

I seem to remember another patient at the other end of the ward, his bed surrounded by visitors. He was looking over at me in disgust at the exhibition I was making of myself. It felt like my body was shutting down, one programme at a time, a bit like my computer does. My "start menu" was vanishing, and the question that began to emerge was - would the "screensaver" disappear too?

I wasn't enjoying this one bit, and looked forward to Pam's arrival when she would sort out these doctors and make sure that I got the right medicine. Bringing this whole sorry episode to an end, hopefully! Then, I could get back home and get on with my preparation for next weekend. But, I only have the vaguest memory of meeting her, and of the venue. or of the circumstances of the meeting. And these, later, proved to be at odds with her version of events.

I remember the nurses saying that I would need to get a catheter fitted next day. But I didn't know what that meant, so there was no fear involved. I had no conscious recollection of the catheterisation process, which is perhaps just as well, as I was later to go through the process twice, fully conscious. I can say, with some authority, that it is not for the faint-hearted!

It was around then also, that I had a deep vein thrombosis in my leg. I am assured that this, too, is quite a painful condition. So, I have no regrets about being oblivious to any memories of the treatment received at that time. Although it is definitely there in my medical records, I sometimes think that this whole episode must be a mistake. In fact, nothing to do with me. However, my wife, who was present as a witness at the time in question, assures me that it really did happen. I can only guess at how much stress she must have been carrying throughout all of this. Fortunately, her employers recognised that she had legitimate grounds for compassionate leave and duly gave her the rest of the year off.

The next thing I remember is being in a small room. The window was open and I remember asking Pam, though I don't know how, to close it for security reasons.

Actually, there was a building site next door and I had already seen some "undesirables" among the shadows. But, I didn't want to alarm Pam and make her any more stressed than she seemed to be. At the back of the hospital, the sea came into the shore. And, perhaps unusually, there was one ward that sloped down the shore, and into the sea itself. At full tide it became almost completely covered by water. I was later to spend some time in that ward and got to know it well. To the front of the hospital lay the Fountainbridge area of Edinburgh with a large car parking area, set aside for staff and visitors.

My next memory is of my family, along with Pam, seated around my bed. My body was now completely "frozen" and I drifted in and out of consciousness in what they call "locked-in syndrome." Basically, it meant that I was at home, but couldn't phone out. I had no lateral support from the muscles in the side of my body which meant that if I started to lean in one direction I had no way of correcting things. Nor did I have any tummy muscles available to me, which meant that I couldn't sit up. All in all, you could be forgiven for thinking that I had pretty much turned into the proverbial beached whale!

As I overheard one nurse putting it, I had been like the Man from Del Monte and had now turned into a large blob of uselessness.

At the time, I noticed that this nurse had obviously got his knowledge about my previous lifestyle from another source, but it didn't unduly concern me from where. Surprise, surprise, I was thinking much the same thing! I was alone in there, as much, perhaps as Brian Keenan had been during his period of solitary confinement in Beirut! Judging from the glum expressions on the faces all around me, something serious must be up! On leaving, a relative said, "Keep fighting, not just for your sake, but for the sake of the family." I didn't know what it was that I was supposed to be fighting. It didn't feel much like a fight to me. More like an unending nightmare, from which I would hopefully awaken soon, to resume life as I had known it.

It seemed that the third year medical students believed that it was more ethical to put me to sleep, rather than to keep me alive in this state. Accordingly, they had held one of their ritual meetings where they committed to intervene, and to take radical action to bring my life to an end.

This was in direct defiance of the more senior doctors who, in the eyes of the junior doctors, were "mercilessly" committed to keeping me alive.

I spent that night in a glass fronted shop-like building, on the ground floor. I had incessant hiccups. That was both annoying and frustrating for the other patients, and for the staff. So, I was pleased to see lurking in the shadows, a bodyguard complete with rifle. It turned out that he was on loan from Strathclyde where he usually worked, because Lothian NHS recognised how real the threat to me was.

Next night, I was taken to a more old-fashioned ward, close to the shoreline. I was left in the care of a sister and a young male nurse. They wasted no time. As soon as my Mother and my sister left at the end of visiting time, they strung me up to a pole and began to force feed me through the grey feeding tube that ran up my nose. The idea was to fill me with a silicon solution cunningly disguised as milk. Then, when I was completely full of this silicon, I would be a puppet in their hands, to mould into whatever shape they wanted! My only chance of survival was to keep focusing on my identity and to determinedly resist their attempts to fill me with this liquid!

I remember a session with Pam where she kept encouraging me to "open those beautiful blue eyes." She had never mentioned anything about my eyes before so I wondered why she said it now. Very strange! I noticed also that she had a single strand of grey hair to the right of her face.

She used to take great pride in not having one strand of grey on her head. I wondered if there was something that she knew, something that I didn't. It seemed as though I wasn't supposed to live much longer!

It turns out that that there was something that she knew. And something which I didn't. The medical staff had taken her aside, I was to learn much later, and had told her that they thought that there was so little brain activity that I would only have a very mundane quality of life. They argued that the sensible thing to do, in the circumstances, was to agree that, should my condition continue to deteriorate further, they would not revive me.

You can imagine how Pam reacted to this news! She defiantly reminded them that, as far she was concerned, it was the law of the land that she, and she alone, was able to make these decisions. The ward doctors explained that it was normal for people in her situation to be initially, in denial, but that nevertheless it was a reality that she would have to come to accept eventually. In typical warrior style, Pam set about challenging this version of events, in circumstances where many would have just laid down, in the face of medical opinion.

For my part, there never was any doubt about my faculties being unchanged. I "felt" like the same person. I reasoned in the same way. I had the same values.

Fortunately for me, I was able to go ahead with my modular workshop over the next weekend. I was transferred to a very small hospital in Leith. There were only about four of us in that ward and, fortunately, my clothes, including my car keys, were in a grey steel cabinet at the bottom of my bed. The nurse was fine about me going on weekend leave, and I then set out to deliver my workshop, albeit that I had to get a friend to write on the flip chart.

The event itself was held in a large space reminiscent of an aircraft hanger. Somewhat to my surprise, the size of the group was significantly up on what it had been. I think news of my recent illness had got round, and, recognising that this might be there last chance to get my take on events, they had decided to come along and see what it was all about, even though it was the final module of the course.

I don't remember any details of how I travelled to and from this workshop. It was this lack of continuity, an inability to link these disparate scenes together, that convinced me later that they were mere imaginings. Even though, for me, they are stored in my memory bank, and are just as real as anything else that is stored there.

I discovered that both patients and nurses congregated for midnight meditation sessions on the top floor. I was still going through my hiccup phase, so I was quite a distraction for those assembled in the room. The group made no secret of their frustration with me, and I remember being surprised at, what I considered to be, their rather shallow approach to spirituality.

Around this time, doctors used to awaken me regularly and flash torches in my eyes. It's remarkably intrusive to be woken like this all through the night, with a bright light and a complete stranger looking into your eyes. A lot of them were third-year medical students.

Frankly, I was a bit wary of them. But they were on their best behaviour, under the noses of the consultants. Butter wouldn't melt in their mouths!

I don't recollect a lot about this time. All of my body was "frozen." In fact, I was to discover much later, my entire body was paralysed. It felt like "freezing," from the inside because all my limbs were still there, they had just "seized up". There was not a sense of any limbs being cold but, from the inside, the "frozen" analogy seemed to fit the circumstances quite well. I didn't know anything about the "disease" that I had contracted. But, from what little I could glean, it seemed that eventually my limbs would "defrost" and return to normal.

In these circumstances, Pam and I were forced to devise a means of communication. I suppose it must have been her suggestion because I, certainly, was in no position to devise anything! We followed the time-worn tradition of Pam reciting the alphabet and me blinking when she came to the appropriate letter. Anyone who has tried this will know how frustrating this can be. The partner almost invariably gets tired reciting the same alphabet over and over, and so the menu is usually speeded up making it extremely difficult to blink at the right letter. Added to that, there was the impact of the drugs. They had a soporific effect on me as I was waiting for the appropriate letter to come round. And, once off on a wild goose chase we would both become very frustrated with one another, mirroring the volatility that had always been an undercurrent of our relationship. I dare say Pam didn't find it a bundle of laughs either!

As a child, I had always been deeply bothered by a saying that stood on top of the mantelpiece in my grandparents' house. It said, "Women, you can't live with them, you can't live without them." To my innocent mind as a child this sounded completely illogical, evidence that senility was taking control of my grandparents. But, in these moments, I could understand the dilemma completely!

Strangely, the first of these tortured communications took place in an old fashioned ward. There was a long wooden counter running right down the full length of the room. Behind this, the nurses were going about their routine business. My bed was next to a raised dais and, uncommonly for a hospital, the raised area was concealed behind a thick red curtain. There was something else going on that involved this curtain, but I can't remember what it was.

Pam, knowing my, hitherto, keen interest in rugby casually asked, who won the honour of being Scottish "man of the match" in the most recent international match?" With Pam reciting the alphabet, I blinked out, correctly, the name of "Sean Lamont." While, for me this conversation had been no big deal, for Pam it was the first clear evidence that she had that I still had some control over my mental faculties. Something she had been warned by the doctors not to expect. She went back, triumphantly, to report this development to the ward doctors. Much later, I was to discover that she was met with some medical scepticism. She was warned that spouses often took false hopes from events and that it was time to start accepting the inevitable.

There just wasn't enough brain activity to support this kind of communication!

It was about this time that my love affair with physiotherapy began. The physios instructed me to move parts of my anatomy. They could see what others had missed, micro-movements in the appropriate muscles. They duly reported this back to the doctors who were forced to change their position. It's at times like this that you find out who your friends are!

This was the beginning, but certainly not the end, of our disillusionment with the medical treatment on offer! Already, Pam and I were starting to participate in a dark nightmare in which the two of us conspired together against, what we characterised at the time, as a fairly hostile and cumbersome, NHS. Having subsequently spoken at length to some of the doctors involved with acute stroke care, I am now satisfied that they are an intelligent and well-motivated group of people. At the time though, I think we both took the view that I had survived a serious stroke, but now followed the much more arduous task of surviving inside a much more dangerous beast, the NHS.

The visual alertness of the physios was a significant breakthrough because it meant that the full weight of the rehabilitation process started to kick in behind me. I think we both interpreted this, at the time, as some kind of "victory" over the medical establishment whose authority was now open to challenge in a way that would have been unthinkable, just a few months earlier.

Perhaps fortunately, I don't remember much about these early days. There is a generalised impression of being uncomfortable in bed. It was ward policy to turn patients once during the morning and once more during the afternoon. I obviously can't talk for anyone else. But, after about forty minutes, I became uncomfortably stiff and so found the ward policy to be totally inadequate for my needs. In its worst form, this generalised stiffness would become localised cramps, usually in my legs. It is difficult to exaggerate the terror of having cramp when you are totally in silence and your whole body is "frozen" in the way that mine was. Cramp, is an intensely social condition. We are generally very effective at signalling the state of distress that comes with the onset of cramp. And, we're skilled, too, at coming immediately to the assistance of someone displaying signs of cramp. This was the world that I had grown accustomed to. So, imagine being "frozen" in a motionless body and, at the same time, unable to verbalise the pain! The terror of these situations was as bad as the pain itself! Now, it is an almost daily occurrence, but the fear of cramps has dissipated.

Without the medium of language, and with a curtailed programme of body language, expressing myself on health-related matters became a curiously analogue affair. I was either ill or not ill. The grey area that exists between these polarities, the digital scale that I had grown used to, was no longer available to me. Several years later, I was to call for an ambulance, by means of my support workers, only to be told to get someone to call back again if I lost consciousness. Seems I was not alone in thinking in terms of polarities!

There were drips on either side of me, one filled with crystal clear water, and the other with a bag of liquid feed which was dripped into me via a grey feeding tube over about a ten hour period.

This was the bag into which they would introduce silicon. It even took on another colour if it had been doctored. They thought I wouldn't notice, but I did!

Every so often, a curious metallic "ping" would ring out to notify everyone that the drip, of whatever it was, was finished. This continued day and night, and with an average response time of about fifteen minutes. Needless to say, it was quite a noisy environment! And there was an endless string of nurses doings "obs." This involved sticking temperature gauges in my ears at approximately hourly intervals and then fitting a blood pressure monitor on my arm. The equipment they used as their instruments of torture were mounted on a trolley that made a distinctive rattling noise as it was pushed up the corridor. I knew that when I heard that sound, it meant that I was destined to go through the whole rigmarole yet again.

Then there were the phlebotomists! I swear, at one point, they were forming an orderly queue at the bottom of my bed, as they waited their turn to take samples of my blood. On one occasion, there were three young doctors who tried, one after the other, for a total of eighteen times, to get a blood sample. Each doctor told me, in conspiratorial tones, that they were only supposed to try twice, inferring that I should be grateful that they were really pushing the boat out for me! And, in case you're wondering, this, sadly, is part of my story not a flight of fancy! I had a visitor at the time that was a witness to this little adventure!

As I have indicated above, feeding was through a grey tube that ran up my nose, and down my throat. Over time, my left nostril began to block. It was to be months later before I was in a position to unblock it, and, understandably, none of the nursing staff seemed up for this level of intimacy!

I began to lose muscle mass and I remember one of the nurses referred to me as "chicken legs," which was the first time that I realised that my body might be going through changes that were completely outwith my sphere of influence. This might be seen as a minor issue, but my legs, at the time, along with the rest of my body, formed a part of my "identity," my sense of "self".

It was years later, before I was able to come to terms with the fact that my identity had inevitably been changed by the recent course of events. I may have stayed the same on the inside, but I sure as hell was presenting myself differently on the outside!

My frozen left arm had a tag on it that indicated clearly that the useless arm with fingers that were now almost permanently clenched into a tight ball, was due to be replaced on the eighth of April. What concerned me most was that I had heard through the grapevine that it was to be replaced by the arm of a ten-year old. I wasn't convinced that it would continue to age. If it didn't, then I would be left with the arm of a ten-year old for the rest my life, (which, for all I knew, might not be very long!)

I remember that, around this time, it was announced on the radio that Pope John Paul had fallen into a coma and wasn't expected to come out of it alive. Now, I am not a Roman Catholic, and have never been one. But his dilemma seemed to mirror mine. For a moment in time, we became almost brothers, and I wondered which of the two of us would leave the scene first. I remember also, being very moved by the news of his death a few days later; in a way that no one on the outside would know about or even understand. It seemed that my name would be called another day!

I remember being surprised too at how my nurses responded to my silence! In some instances they ignored me as they worked on my frozen body, and just chatted to each other as though I wasn't there. In this way, I gained access to a lot of information that I would otherwise be denied. In other instances, they would act as though I was deaf, and mime out a little scenario for me. They seemed curiously thrown by my circumstances, which I found strange in an acute stroke ward. I was later to discover that there had only been two cases of brain-stem strokes admitted to that hospital in recent history. So, perhaps they were just not used to particular symptoms that I was presenting!

Without claiming any medical expertise whatsoever, it seems from my experience that a conventional stroke tends to affect the ability of patients to reason, and sometimes also the memory, as well as usually causing some measure of physical disability. With brain-stem strokes it tends to be a little bit different. The ability to reason remains intact, as do the social skills. But what is massively affected is the ability to communicate, as well as the loss of motor skills such as walking. And so, brain-stem stroke patients tend to be very different animals than other stroke patients, albeit that both groups face daunting challenges!

By listening in on these discussions, I got a "feel" for the office politics of the ward and, being a business consultant, would think the issues through in my head, designing what I considered to be, some appropriate ways to intervene and to start to turn things around. Actually, when I thought about it, it was an excellent way (though perhaps a bit extreme) to get a real insight about what was going, at least at the sharp end of hospital services. It's just a shame that no one appeared to be in listening mode, a big deficiency in the NHS. I don't know whom they listen to, maybe to each other! But it is clear that patients are there solely as the recipients of medical lectures and certainly not as "clients" with feelings, and opinions, worth listening to.

By a strange quirk of fate, I had previously done some consultancy work for an NHS Trust. So, although I had seen some of these issues before, they had never been so well defined as they appeared now. I obviously can't refer to information I gathered in confidence, but my previous exposure did alert me to some of the issues round about me now.

My wife used to put music on before she left the hospital each day. There were two albums in particular that featured heavily around this time. One was "Snow Patrol's" invitation to, "Light up, light up," with its curious message "I am still with you, even though you may not hear my voice." It was the song that I had repeatedly played during breaks on my last training course, and which now seemed strangely prescient.

In it, there is a curious mixture of sadness and happiness. Before, I had wondered how well the sad undertone fitted in to the general pattern of, what I found to be, a very uplifting theme. But now, the song seemed just right for the situation in which I now found myself! It never failed to bring me to floods of tears, as befitted my newly developed emotional persona.

The other was "Keane's" album, which had been gifted to me by one participant in that last group that I'd been working with, (if you're out there Andrew, I haven't forgotten that kindness.) In it, is the line "I'll see you on the other side," which I took as a coded message from Pam. It struck me as a very clever way to pass on a very difficult message. It seemed that she was prepared for the worst. Another track from this album, which seemed to be speaking straight at me, was, "Everybody's changing, but I don't feel the same."

Around this time also, I heard a current release by Michael Bublé. I remember thinking that the ease with which he delivered his song was like the missing link in my life. All of my life, I had been involved in the relentless march towards the next pinnacle and there had been several monsters to slay along the way! But, no matter how many windmills were behind me, there always seemed to be another on the horizon. Looking back on it now, it had been a warrior's life! But maybe, at some point, it would have been good to have lied back occasionally and have had a Michael Bublé moment!

I don't regret the life choices that I made, barring a few ill-judged ones. But, it had been pretty full on, and there did seem to have been a fair amount of struggle along the way. To support this train of thought, I had yet another of my "experiences."

This time, I was in Nazi headquarters somewhere. I was being tortured as a consequence of my overt resistance to the regime. I remember the excruciating pain of having my knee twisted, right round, and wondering if there was any political principle that was worth this amount of agony!

I was definitely questioning the very basis upon which my life had been based and the characteristics that had made me, me. It was a moment of taking stock and of evaluating my life's direction.

On a much more mundane level, I also remember the arrival on the ward of the teas and the meals. I watched enviously as the other stroke patients gathered round the trolley and exchanged pleasant-ries. It was my first feeling of social exclusion, but not my last. It's funny how these informal gatherings hold little significance until they are made "off-limits".

Often the nurses would chatter about how they were "going to murder their breakfast," during an up-coming break. I would have dearly love to have joined them, if I were able! I regarded having a cup of tea now, as a real "privilege." An opportunity to enjoy some meaningless banter. And, I wondered how long it might be, before I was up and able to take my place amongst them?

I was thinking in terms of days, let alone weeks, months, or years. And, I yearned for some extreme taste to stimulate my taste buds and provide some contrast to this tasteless concoction they kept pumping into me. It may have been saving my life but there was no way that I felt gratitude, at the time! In fact, at this stage of my illness, I would have gladly have wasted away, given the opportunity. But, I was not! (You may be getting some confusing mixed messages about whether I wanted to live or die. This varied at different stages, but I remained adamant that it was a decision that I should take, not doctors or nurses!)

So the drama continued, day after horrific day! Perhaps the most surprising thing to me, at this time, was that I reversed my normal pattern of seeing myself through the eyes of others. Just look at the start of this story, and notice how often I checked to consider how others might feel about a specific scenario. It was, pretty much, the basis of how I worked in businesses. But that behaviour was now reversed. Now, everything seemed to rotate around me.

I don't know the mechanics of this but I had it fixed in my mind that people passing my room door were only there for my entertainment. Nobody had a life to get on with other than to be bit-players in my drama. Looking back on it now, it seems like an incredibly arrogant proposition. When, finally, I did hit the streets, it was something of a shock to me to find that the world had continued to spin, and that people had moved on with their lives. I had probably expected that the world had stopped and had been in some form of limbo for the last couple of years. Initially, it was very difficult for me to accept that most people had just got on with their lives, and that others had departed the scene altogether. It must be something similar to the experience of a prisoner returning to his community, and finding it a changed place.

One morning, the consultant swept down the corridor with his usual bevy of attendants in his wake. They all stopped at my door and in the midst of his talk I heard the consultant refer to my "periodic episodes of paranoia." I remember the instant retort inside my head, the classic, "Just because I'm paranoid, it doesn't mean they're not out to get me!" And I remember thinking of how his tone would soon change if he had any inkling of what was happening under his very nose! When the bevy eventually made its way into my room it was clear from their darting eyes that the primary focus of their attention was on each other. It seemed that they were jealously vying for the consultant's attention and that, as a result, they were really not really interested in connecting with me.

It was about this time that I discovered that there was a plot among five of the nurses to continue with the plan of force-feeding me with silicon via my feeding tube. One of them, in fact, got admitted as a patient in order to get closer to me. He kept changing his first name in order to confuse me, but he followed me as I moved from ward to ward, and seemed to be getting some insider information about my whereabouts in the hospital. He was never far behind me.

I tried to alert Pam to this violence, but not seeing what was going on, she dismissed it as "absurd!" I got half the way through spelling out the names of the conspirators when she threw her hands up in the air. "Look, this is getting ridiculous! No one's trying to kill you!" What could I do? My own wife was not taking me seriously!

It was around this time that "William" was wheeled out. "William," was a Church of Scotland Minister who had been a participant on one of my last training courses? He was familiar with the big questions of life and death and was quite confident in asking them. Little did I know, at the time, that he had been briefed by Pam and was tasked to get the answers to some pretty fundamental questions like, "Do you want to carry on living, Stuart?" This wasn't something I had consciously given much thought to.

But, after the question was put to me, I ran quickly through the content of my life to date. Yes, when I thought about it there were still projects that I wanted to finish, and places that I still wanted to visit. Nepal and Patagonia, for example. And New Zealand.

On balance, I thought it best to stay and pick up where I had left off. To continue down the highway, and discover what other surprises lay ahead. Especially if that future involved getting back together with Pam, in some format or other, as seemed likely. It did not occur to me that I would now be proceeding down an entirely different route with some very strange terrain, some very odd landmarks!

Had I been aware of the extent to which my experience was to be degraded, as a consequence of my strokes, it would have been a much more difficult question to answer. I noticed that William didn't mention the Pope's death, an event that had assumed great significance in my rather confused mind. Knowing William as I do, this event would have registered on his map too. He probably just considered it inappropriate as a topic for an acute stroke ward. But, William had another important piece to contribute. And this time it proved to be something of a "master-stroke!" You could say the "Mother of All Strokes!"

The problem which, unknown to me, both he and my wife had jointly discussed was how to make life a little more tolerable in an environment that I was clearly experiencing, rightly or wrongly, as "life-threatening".

This was not going to be easy for them as I had witnessed things as being "real," through my trusted senses and was, at the time, adamant that these, previously reliable senses, were presenting me with an accurate version of events.

The strategy that they came up with is one that I might have used myself, in similar circumstances. It was a double bind. "William" reminded me that one of the central planks of my training had been the notion that, given their life experience, and the limited amount of strategic options available to them at the time, people invariably make the best choices possible. In other words, in normal circumstances, their decision-making remains rooted in rationality. Maybe it might not seem like this on the following day, or years later. But, at the time, it did! Of course we may have done something that, with hindsight, appears pretty stupid! But, if you think about it, there was never a time in your life when you thought, X would be the best option so I'll choose to do Y! No, you chose Y because it appealed to you more, for whatever reason, at the time.

I remember hearing about a conversation with one of the trainers off the oil-rig platform, Piper Alpha. He refuted the idea that the men on that platform had made the best decision available to them during the blaze on that platform. They had been trained to go through a door and turn in a certain direction, in order to head away from any likely fire. Instead of going through that door and turning away from the fire, as they had been trained, they had turned in a direction that took them directly towards the fire. Consequently, he argued, they had not made the best decision available to them!

In fact, I think it illustrates the point very well! I find it hard to imagine a circumstance where the men went through the door, and said to themselves, "If we head in this direction we'll head towards safety, so let's head in the opposite direction that'll take us towards the fire."

We can safely assume that, for some reason, the men chose to go in the direction that appeared to them, at that time, and in those circumstances, to offer the best prospect of safety. We can only speculate on the factors that were pertinent to them in reaching that fateful decision. However, we can safely assume that, being rational human beings, they did what they believed to be the wisest thing to do, at the time. No matter how flawed it may appear with the benefit of hindsight.

So, now "William" was turning my teaching back on me. Either I could contradict my earlier teaching, or apply it to my present circumstances, in the hospital. In a situation where I believed that my very life was at stake, it was not easy to take my own medicine. Nevertheless I was forced by William's " intervention" to admit that the nurses who were caught up in the conspiracy must all be doing so because, from their perspective, it seemed like the most sensible thing to do, or else contradict a central plank of my earlier training.

This was a key piece for me because I could see in it a logic that, for me, transcended issues of life and death and removed for the first time since that fateful first day, that unspoken sense of grievance that had been festering inside. Since my arrival in hospital I had unconsciously been using the mantra made famous by that actor in the

"Injurylawyers4U" TV advert. "I, absolutely, did not deserve this!" Victimhood did not sit easily on my shoulders!

That intervention from "William" probably marked the beginning of my comeback. For the first time in my illness, I realised that I was well placed to design "ecological," effective, strategies for dealing with the various hurdles that were apparent all around me.

In my business life, I had been responsible for helping executives in big national companies to develop strategies, which had a win/win/win structure. Now, I had the opportunity to put all that learning into practice! I quickly decided for example that the suspicious glares I had been giving to anyone who went near my feeding tube, was not an accurate expression of how I wanted to be. I made a conscious decision to start building relations with the nursing staff (even if my repertoire was still limited.) Rather than as hitherto, waiting to see if the other person was willing to dance with me!

The force-feedings were to continue, and they still filled me with terror when they occurred, but, at some level, things had changed.

I still regarded it as a rather sordid little game they were playing. But, now saw that they were acting in accordance with their model of how the world works. I got that they didn't know any better. I was back with that Brian Keenan point, of all those years ago. I had the power to choose my state whereas these bullies didn't have a choice. They were just driven by their hatred!

Chapter 3 Back down the highway

All of the events mentioned in this chapter really did happen. And no, these do not stem from a recurrence of my paranoid delusions. I have the photos to prove most of them. Although, I have organised and presented these experiences to the best of my ability, I accept that the sequence may have got slightly distorted over the years. If so, I apologise. There certainly was no deliberate attempt to mislead. I include this here as the events mentioned in this chapter had a pro-found effect on the rest of my life and on whom I subsequently "believed my self to be."

Stepping out into that fierce sunlight was like a blast from an open furnace. This was my third trip to India, but my first via Afghan Air-ways and my first stop over in Kabul. The year was 1978. From the air it had not looked very promising. Little mounds of dried mud raised out of a landscape, made up of more brown mud. This was as severe an environment as I had encountered!

With some trepidation about what we had let ourselves in for, just to save a few pounds on our air ticket, we descended from the aircraft, and made our way to the airport terminal. The terminal was memora-ble because, unlike most terminals throughout the world, it was devoid of any merchandise. Even at the "bar area" there was only a selection of soft drinks and a few bowls of pistachio nuts. All around the inside of the terminal building there were very large photos of moustachioed men, presumably, the political elite. Their unsavoury portraits domi-nated the room, and did nothing to lighten the atmosphere.

It was with a measure of relief that we re-boarded the plane a couple of hours later. We were headed towards Delhi with its much more conventional airport and its teeming masses, and aggressive entrepre-neurship, at every turn. From there, there was a three-day train jour-ney to Rajasthan, followed by a coach journey, up to the hill station, that was my final destination.

There was not much of note happening on the train journey, apart from the ever-changing vista, and the endless chorus as we pulled into yet another station, of "Chai, garam chai, " from the thousands of tea sellers dotted around India, day and night. There were also forlorn looking mothers, invariably holding babies, their hands poking through the open windows, together with pitiful cries of "Buckshee." What made it worse was the awareness that, for many, these noisy, chilly platforms were also what they called home.

There was also an interesting (in my opinion) conversation that I had with a man in the same compartment. A propos nothing, he suddenly blurted out, "You are looking like officer class!"

There was a slight inflection in his voice that led me to believe that this was a question that required some kind of an answer, rather than merely a statement of what he saw before him. I was wearing the robes of a yogi at the time, which was probably at least responsible for his curiosity.

We did not refer to ourselves as monks, but led lives of celibacy and lived lives in such a rigorous regime that we would have put most monks to shame. So, for ease of communication, I often now describe myself as having been a "yogic monk." This is a much simpler term to convey the full meaning of living a yogic lifestyle. It is certainly not meant to mislead anyone. Amongst Western intellectuals, there seems to be a spectrum of religions. And, it seems that Buddhist monasticism falls at the more socially acceptable end of the spectrum. So, no matter how many times I try to clarify the situation, friends continue to introduce me as "a former Buddhist monk." Ah, well, different strip, but they play in the same league!

In the West, it is often held to be true that there is only one form of yoga and that involves the contortion of bodies. In fact, there are four main forms of yoga within the traditions of India. There is the one that we're familiar with in the West, involving attempts to **still**

the body, and thus allow the spirit to fly. Then there's the Hare Krishna approach, which aims to achieve a higher state of consciousness by **worship and devotion**. There's also a yogic tradition, involving the in-depth study of the Hindu scriptures, and the constant churning of points of **knowledge**.

But the one that interested me was the fourth yoga, **meditation** on the meaning that lies behind all things. It was not the ponderous Raja Yoga of the past, but Sahaj (easy) Raja involving no complicated rituals and easily accessible no matter which religious background one came from, or even none, like me.

It was not that I had powerful experiences in meditation, because I was a believer. Rather, it was that I was compelled to be a believer, by virtue of the blissful experiences I was having in meditation. I was dragged, screaming and kicking, into the fold of the believers! I did not choose to live a yogic life, it chose me. At the time I was a bright young thing, with my whole colourful future ahead. Submitting to a strict spiritual discipline was the last thing on my mind!

Anyway, the subject under discussion in my railway compartment quickly turned to interpreting the meaning of the Vedas, one of the major scriptures of the Hindu religion. In keeping with many more Asian men I had encountered, he became very authoritative, almost didactive, on the subject of what the scriptures said. It seemed to be part of the male psyche of many Indian men. They would suddenly turn on a pompous authority when the subject turned to Hindu scriptures.

But, when I asked him how much of the scriptures he embodied and lived out of, he gave me a non-committed look, rolled his hand in an indecisive rocking gesture. He eventually broke out into an embarrassed smile that seemed to suggest that surely it was enough to spout this stuff! If he was typical of many of the men I had met on my travels in India he would view the living of a spiritually disciplined life as being strictly for Holy Men and "paramatmas," the great souls. And certainly not for the likes of him, a mere "householder! "

Our conversation had drawn some attention. There were a few souls that obviously understood what was being discussed and who smiled broadly at the man's rapidly deflating bubble. But the majority of the assembled onlookers clearly had no idea what was being discussed and were merely staring open-mouthed at what was a very unusual sight on a train journey.

Such gatherings of curious onlookers were an oddly endearing quality of daily Indian life. It didn't matter if it was a collapsed body, or a car crash. Both would provide the excuse for a large crowd to gather. And there would be no furtive looks either, like the ones you get from passing vehicles at the scene of a motorway crash in Britain! These would be full-blown stares from a stationary and rooted circle of on-lookers.

Life in the ashram where I was due to be staying was tough by most people's standards. The day started with loud music to waken us, at 3.30a.m. This was a call to morning meditation at 4a.m. One thousand people would gather together in the meditation hall to lay the founda-tions for the day. Then, at 5a.m., we would start the business of morn-ing ablutions in time for the start of morning class at 6a.m. We're not talking about holiday facilities here. We're talking about holes in the ground and buckets of cold water. What made this a tricky business were the absence of any mirrors in the ashram, and the process of shaving with cold water. All of the yogis were clean-shaven. This was encouraged, though not required, as an outward symbol of our disci-plined way of life.

Morning class, in which we would churn philosophy and meditate on how specifically that philosophy might impact on our plans for the day, last-ed till 8a.m. We were encouraged to set outcomes for the day, and then later to evaluate our success, all of which information we volun-tarily handed in to our teachers so that they were aware of the personal battles we were engaged in. After breakfast we had a couple of hours for personal shopping or laundry. There was a dhobiwalah located in the nearby village, to whom we entrusted our white "pyjamas" and shawls.

At about 11a.m. we began our karam yoga, our meditation in action. Feeding one thousand yogis and yoginis was not going to be a simple task!

We set about the task in silence, by each wading through a mountain of vegetables, or by sifting through a pile of pulses. When our jobs were completed about an hour later, we would head back to our living quarters knowing that our host cooks would convert our raw materials into something edible, in their large cauldrons. Lunch was the same every day to encourage us to think about it as no more than a pit stop for the body, during which essential fuel would be taken onboard.

After lunch we took a well-earned siesta or went shopping in the village. Often there were clothes to be collected in the afternoon from the dhobiwallah. Afternoon class usually began at 4p.m. during which, we would regurgitate the day's theme and meditate further. And that took us nicely into dinner. As at lunchtime, we would take this seated, silently in long rows, cross-legged on the dusty ground. The ashram residents would walk down the line, armed with buckets of dhal, or chapatis, or subjee (a mixture of local vegetables, usually featuring

potato and aubergines.) In the evening we would have another class, which would often turn into cultural exchanges, involving inputs from different regions of the globe. At 10p.m. there would be urns dispensing hot milk and then our lights went out about 11p.m. ready for it all to begin again next morning.

A guard, dressed in full military regalia protected the ashram. I remember approaching the guard one evening, in worried tones. I reported that I had just seen a rat disappear up a drainpipe in my building.

To my amazement, the guard responded by rocking his head from side to side in a gesture that expressed his complete marvel at the beauty of it all. He then beamed back a smile of blissfulness and said, "Oh very nice, very nice," in a voice that seemed be saying, "Don't tell the others, they'll all be wanting one!"

To this day, I don't know if he understood me and was just reframing the situation with immense skill, or whether we had just got our wires crossed! Certainly, this place was redolent with yogis who had amazing perspectives, on all sorts of issues.

A photo, showing me with some of the residents of the ashram at this time is shown in Appendix 1, Fig. 1.

During this trip, I was asked twice to go to the gatehouse to explain matters to English speakers who had dropped in at the front gate out of curiosity, and in order to find out what the ashram was all about. On the first occasion it was a man that I had wrestled with many times when we were children at school, in Edinburgh. He "just happened" to be passing with, presumably, his partner and their young baby son, in a pushchair. In primary school I had led a long line of trotting "knights" around the playground, two by two, in the manner of Sir Lancelot, (as in the T.V. series, of the same name, which featured at the time, a young Roger Moore.) Duly replete with moral zeal, we were searching for some injustice to correct. Invariably, that involved Tottie Andy's gang! In my mind, at that time, they were the very embodiment of evil. Tottie Andy himself was too small to fight his own battles so he would appoint a henchman to fight on his behalf. I only ever remember winning these encounters, but admit that selective memory may be at work here!

And now, some twenty years down the line, I was seated in an ashram, located on a hill station, on the top of mountain, some three days' train journey through the Rajasthan desert and facing that very henchman!

So that old relationships and ties did not tug us backwards and into old habits we were encouraged to view our pasts as "previous lives". At first sight, this might set alarm bells ringing in the West where the family unit is so sacrosanct. But how many of my readers would welcome the opportunity to start again, with a clear slate? The French Foreign Legion is not the only option!

To return now to the ashram. In my eyes, I was effectively coming face to face with someone from a previous life. And, with this frame of mind, I was able to run through the ashram's objectives without delving into our joint history of a warring past. I didn't even acknowledge that we had a shared past which allowed me to remain detached. With hindsight though it may have seemed quite a strange meeting to him! Not that I was unduly concerned about that!

The second visitor was an eighty-year old American man named "Frank." He was staying in the area for a few days. He claimed to be a millionaire but I had no way of verifying that. In any case, he had arrived at the one place in the world where his wealth didn't cut the mustard. He came for lessons on about three days running. On each occasion, he trailed his money before me as though that would alter my perception of him. And then he moved off, never to be seen again, on my Indian journeys!

As the last paragraph suggests we did a fair amount of travel. A lecture tour of Central India had been organised for about six of us Westerners on the grounds that our message might be heard more effectively than that of our Indian brothers, who might be seen as representatives in India of a by-gone era. Many of our audience were actively "dreaming the dream," in an India that was on the cusp of economic parity with the major players. We had lived the dream and had found it lacking. It was hoped that we could make use of our experience of already having lived that "dream" to persuade at least some that it was not all it was cracked up to be! In this way, we hoped that we could prevent some from having to find this out, the hard way. Of course, I had all the usual reservations about proselytising! But, that was far outweighed by the opportunity to prevent considerable suffering.

Strangely, I had started this campaign way back in my career as a radical socialist, concerned about the excesses of capitalism and the ever-increasing gap between rich and poor. It was only the violent squabbling amongst my socialist flatmates, usually over girlfriends and, during which, curiously proprietorial tendencies would emerge, that convinced me that maybe what was needed was a holistic initiative, that addressed moral issues as well as some of the more obvious issues. Maybe it was the constant "liberation" of my food from the fridge, always carried out anonymously, that finally pushed me over the edge!

Whist this leap across the metaphysical divide might strike some people as odd, for me it was the same end, truth, just another strategy. But, I emphasise it was not a leap I could, or would, have made on my own. I was carried across the gap in an effortless shift.

Meanwhile, back on the lecture tour, I found myself falling into the trap of indulging in a little pedagogy! Whilst delivering yet another talk, I had, inadvertently, begun to wander down the same path as some of the Indian men that I have previously referred to in this chapter. I was beginning the talk with some authority on the subject of Hindu philosophy. My host at the event, reached over with a little note, politely asking me to start talking about my vices! Life has a way of deflating you when your bubble gets too big!

Incidentally, when I was feeding this tale back to my senior teacher back in London, herself an Indian, she was not amused that Westerners had been used in this way. She was strongly of the view that, by asking us to concentrate on our vices, our local host was inadvertently dragging down our consciousness. In her opinion, that wouldn't help anyone!

Someone must have alerted the press corps as to our itinerary because they were waiting at each station as we circled the Madya
Pradesh area.

I take it that they were representatives from some local rag because
they asked inane questions like, "Come on, admit it. Isn't it just these
pretty young girls in saris that attracted you to this way of life?"

The tour went quite well, with audiences of about two hundred at most
venues, though I don't know how effective we were in persuading people to give up the materialist dream. Fig. 2 shows me mid-lecture in
Bhopal, shortly after receiving my written rebuke.

Three things stand out in my memory of this trip. First, there was a
tour of a pharmaceuticals plant in one town. I think it was Bhopal.
During the tour, we passed what looked like three medium-sized swim-
ming pools filled with a black tar-like substance. When I asked

what it was our guide said, matter-of-factly, "Oh, this is where we dry
our opium? Most of our medicines contain some opiate." We were told
that if someone accidentally slipped into the storage tanks, and then
ingested some of the opium it is likely that they would die, such was
purity of the opium on display. I don't know if this is accepted as
strictly scientifically true, but in any case, it served as an effective
disincentive to trespassers. I was touched to be sufficiently trusted
by virtue of my role as a yogi, or "holy man," to be given such a privileged tour of these high security facilities. I had never before been
trusted to this extent and it felt very privileged.

The second memory that I have is of making a visit to an Indian prison.
I don't remember where it was precisely or what it was called. Only
that it was where most of the imprisoned "Dacoits" were held. I think
it was somewhere in Madya Pradesh. The "Dacoits" were a group of
Indian brigands who were notorious at the time. As I recall them,
they were a group of outlaws that would show up in large groups of

around one hundred and completely take over a village, or a small town! Such was their confidence that they would even engage local forces in shoot-outs, and usually came out on top! They did so knowing that they could melt away into the jungle when things started to get really nasty. The Dacoits, were led by a bandanna-wearing woman. In Asian culture this was remarkable! She herself had been the recipient of much abuse and corruption from the so-called "authorities." She viewed her campaign as a sort of "Robin Hood" affair, stealing from the rich and giving to the poor.

I remember walking across the prison exercise yard and, like most scenes in India, it was crowded with men dressed in white pyjamas. As we made our way towards a plinth the crowd parted ahead of us. It was like the parting of the Red Sea. I'm not sure that they knew who we were but they could probably guess from our clothes and general demeanour that we were "VIPs" of some sort, and possibly, that we were "holy men and women". In India, at least at that time, the status of "holy man" generated a great deal of respect, even from amongst the ranks of the younger generation, which was just coming to terms with a new level of consumerism. Things may have changed now.

Their mood was one of eager anticipation as we mounted the platform. I suppose, if nothing else, it would break up their day! I remember beginning by building rapport with my audience. I started by saying what seemed to me to be true, that we had all broken the law at some stage in our lives. I continued by suggesting that they were just the unlucky ones, the ones who had got caught. This generated a huge roar of approval once it was translated. It seemed that I had struck a chord! From this perspective, we were all in a cell prisoners of our limited consciousness. In so far as all this was true, I suggested that their prison accommodation provided them with an ideal place for meditation, free from the distractions of everyday life and so enabling them to break out of their individual mental "cells." So, I said that what I wanted to see in that prison was a "mass breakout!" But of the kind that the guards would be happy to see also! I don't recall any more of that visit but I liked to think that at least one life was touched that day!

My third memory is quite different, though it is again set somewhere in Madya Pradesh, I think, in the small town of Bikanir. It involves the local yoga centre where we were sleeping on the current stage of our lecture tour. One morning as we were seated at the kitchen table of that local centre a pile of chapatis was laid on a window-sill adjacent to the breakfast table. Suddenly a mouse ran out from behind some books on the windowsill, right along the sill, across the chapatis, and out through a little hole on the opposite side of the windowsill. I was on the case right away.

I summoned the woman in charge of the centre and pointing an accusing finger towards the chapatis explained in a grave voice what I had just seen. "Acha" she said. In English that meant "Okay." She then moved the chapatis to the centre of the breakfast table obviously concerned that this embarrassing incident should not be repeated, at least not in front of her esteemed Western visitors. Like the rat incident I mentioned before, it put into context the ability we Westerners have to be spooked by the tiniest things, things to which our hosts seemed to be largely indifferent! Left to my own devices I would have had the entire building fumigated and blocked up any holes! As it was, we got an impression of how the centres operate in the smaller townships and how specifically they were tailoring things to deal with local circumstances.

In the West, being in control of one's own destiny is usually regarded as a positive thing whereas, in the East, it is often seen as an obstacle in the process of losing ego consciousness. Alarm bells also rang out amongst some friends and family regarding this same issue. Since the family only knew you through the ego that you had acquired over the years, it was an understandably daunting prospect for them to watch that ego being eroded through the power of yoga!

This visit had lasted several months, into early 1979. It was time to begin the sixteen-hour journey home! The return leg of my flight was also through Afghan Airways, stopping over in Kabul. I had heard vaguely that the Russians had invaded Afghanistan but had not really given much thought to how this might affect everyday life there. It only took a couple of seconds out to find out what was different this time. Once again, I was on the aircraft landing steps in the ferocious Kabul heat.

There, at the bottom of the steps, were two Russian paratroopers. Significantly, their guns were pointed towards us, as opposed to being slung casually over their shoulders. For the first time I knew what it

felt like to look down the barrel of an AK47, or equivalent. And it wasn't a very comfortable feeling! There was a keen intelligence in the eyes of the paratroopers and a strong, rugged muscularity to their physique. But above all, there was a confidence and a steely determination. It was as though they were looking for an excuse to open fire with that slightly psychotic look that is usually portrayed on the faces of power-crazy US troops, in Vietnamese villages.

When we finally made it off the tarmac and into the merciful shelter of the terminal the large political portraits had been removed and only the dust-free outlines remained as testimony to their existence. Who was it that said it was the destiny of all political careers to end in failure? Never mind the pistachio nuts were still there! I don't remember the walk back out to the plane so it must have been pretty uneventful. What I do remember is the grey meat that was served just before an unscheduled stop in Teheran, reminiscent in texture to haggis! I didn't eat any being a committed vegetarian, but the smell was enough to turn my stomach!

The descent was both abrupt and bumpy. At the time, it appeared to be a fairly innocent stop over in which Teheran was just doing us a service. But, on reflection, it seems likely that the Afghans were doing some sort of favour for their Iranian cousins. Certainly, when we landed in Teheran the most intelligent group of cleaners that I have ever seen boarded the plane and proceeded to sweep the floor around the passengers' feet. As they did so their eyes darted menacingly around the faces of the passengers, with little attention going onto what was happening with their hand-brushes and their little dustpans.

Looking back down the thirty interim years, and understanding the collaborative nature of Muslim militancy more completely in recent years, it seems almost certain that we had been boarded by a snatch squad. There again I could be making this collaboration up! (It's happened before!) It is likely that they were intent on identifying any of the Shah's people who might cross Iranian airspace, and who were thus seen as "fair game," for the local Islamic militants.

My stomach was still churning from the twin effects of the smell of the food and the rapid descent. I was in serious danger of throwing up and so of making a spectacle of myself in front of my fellow travellers in the seats around. In desperation, I made my way towards the open exit door which was just in front of me, to the right. For a minute I stood on the platform at the top of the aircraft steps and looked out across the Teheran skyline. It was a modern, industrial skyline quite dissimilar to the bleak skyline we had left behind in Kabul. It occurred to me that, somewhere out there, were the unlucky band of Americans who had unwittingly got caught up in what was described as "the American Hostage Crisis."

In contravention of established diplomatic protocol, Islamist students had taken control of the American embassy in Teheran, holding fifty-two American citizens as hostages in the process. It was big news at the time, undermining President Jimmy Carter's authority over the year and a half the crisis lasted. It was with some relief that the plane took off again. I think it still had its full complement of passengers.

The next thing I remember is descending through the customary fog and rain at Heathrow. One would need to develop a sense of humour to live on an island in the middle of all this! Grey skies and a cold drizzle. And later, seated on the Heathrow train, heading back into Central London, I was amazed at how lush everything seemed, carpeted all around with fields of green, which contrasted, sharply with the dried mud of some of the places I had left behind.

On my return, I set about looking for a job that would finance my next trip to India. There was a vast network of well-placed Indians who were eager to help us find work, primarily for the "good karma" that this would generate in their "spiritual bank account." But, in addition, we had a reputation for being good workers who never threw "sickies" and who were heavily committed to the concept of honesty. It was this last quality that made us particularly well suited to bank work. We were not interested, at the time, in building careers for ourselves. Air ticket money was our primary concern.

It was little surprise then when I was offered the post in an Indian bank as a messenger with responsibilities for collecting and delivering very large cheques, which represented the complicated process by means of which banks are (supposed to be) continually involved in the flux of buying and selling. Most of this financial frenzy took place in the City so I got to know that area quite well. I became familiar with the Golden Mile and with the quaint old offices that many of the older banks chose to trade out of.

So there I was, about six months after my last trip to India, doing my morning routine in the City, when "Frank," whom I had last met on top of the mountain in Rajasthan, suddenly popped into my head. What made this particularly unusual was that he hadn't crossed my mind in any of the preceding months. So, stepping out of some bank which was located in the City I found myself wondering what had become of that elderly man I had met in India. I didn't have long to find out because, as I turned the next corner I bumped right into him.

We exchanged a few pleasantries and then he said that he had intended to get back in touch because he needed someone to carry his bags on his way through the airports during his forthcoming trip to South America, where he was thinking of starting a community. All expenses paid, would I be interested? I said I would run it past the Senior Teacher in London. She was renowned for her extraordinarily powerful meditation, and for her wise counsel.

After due consideration, she suggested that we proceed with our plans. However, there were two conditions that she set.
1) That the full return fare from the States be lodged in my bank account from the very beginning, in case things started to go wrong between us.
2) He was to recognise that I was primarily making this trip to promote my own ideas, and not his.

At the time I thought this was needlessly cautious but subsequent events were to prove her approach to be offering wise advice and it was proof once again of the value of taking her advice.

Frank agreed to these conditions and we finally took off around the end of 1980, first to Miami, which was Frank's hometown. Curiously, I don't remember much about the travelling that was involved in this trip but a few of the main scenes are set out below. I remember deliberately walking through the area of Miami where the Race Riots had taken place only a few months previously. I suppose I wanted to test out my yogic power by walking through "troubled water" in a totally peaceful state. With hindsight, perhaps this resembles the religious fanatic who was widely reported as having stepped into the lions' enclosure at his local zoo in the belief that his faith would protect him and who, of course, was quickly mauled to death.

Anyway, I don't think that my senior teacher in London would have lent her approval to the idea. I'm sure the charge of "egotism" would have appeared somewhere in her response. As it was, there were large groups of about fifty black youths, in big huddles on most corners. All they did as I walked past was shout out "Hey, honky boy, what you doing here?" I suppose it must have been quite a strange sight for them seeing a white man, complete with white pyjamas and wrapped in a white shawl, walking calmly (at least in appearance) through their part of town. Anyway, when I emerged unscathed from that area I confess to being more than a little relieved. I think the distortions in my thinking on this one were beginning to become evident, even to me.

We had taken a room facing out to sea in a fairly run-down hotel in Miami Beach. I was less than impressed with Frank's choice of hotel and it downright appalled me that he obviously intended me to be in his company inside a shared room for twenty-four hours a day. It wasn't that I had "diva" delusions. Just that Frank was quite hard work to be around, and a break from his company seemed desirable from a mental health perspective. This accommodation arrangement was a scenario that I had not even imagined as a possibility, and one that would have been a deal-breaker had it even been contemplated as a possibility back in London. I had assumed that separate rooms would have been perfectly possible if he was as rich as he said he was! Especially as my morning routine was so demanding, and involved lots of early morning manoeuvres!

As it was, I crept down the stairs at 4 a.m., waking the owner who was asleep behind his desk, just as they appear in many black and white American films. I warned the unfortunate man that I would be waking him again at 5 a.m. to get back into the hotel, but this news didn't seem to phase him. When, eventually, I did make it out onto the beach I hunkered down on the cool sand and prepared to start the first of my morning meditations. Then along came a martial artist who set up his stall about twenty feet to my left. He practised in the same place every morning. And together we probably made an awesome team!

In India we had been warned about the "barking dogs" whose noise at night continuously carried up the mountain from the valley below. The point that had been stressed in class was that these "barking dogs," in whatever form they came, were not a distraction from meditation but formed the very content of the meditation itself. In other words, it was not necessary to cut out the sound of the barking dogs, setting up a conflict from the start. Rather, it was possible to incorporate the barking dogs into the meditation. In this way, they would quickly be left behind. My martial artist friend seemed to fit well into the "barking dog" category.

During the days, we met with some of Frank's friends who, like Frank, had chosen to live out their later years in Miami's all-year round sunshine.

But there was a down side to this climate too. I remember sleepless nights when little pools of sweat would gather in the hollow of my chest. And, there was an altogether more sinister side to the weather. For Florida was on the hurricane route. In fact, there was one due in any day now. It had been given the name "Allen" and had been trailed as one of the most devastating ever to come ashore on the coast of Florida. I was actually quite excited at the prospect of seeing out my first hurricane. I had previously only seen them on T.V. There were no instructions to evacuate as there might be today. Just advice to stay off the streets which, in the circumstances, was a bit of a no-brainer. The hurricane itself was very evocative of these old Humphrey Bogart films with palm trees bending right over and random bits of vegetation pressed hard against the window by the driving storm.

Perhaps, if I had seen some of the devastation caused by these hurricanes, to both property and lives, I would have been more afraid than I was. In the event, I was more interested than afraid. After a while, I don't remember how long, the hurricane moved on to new stomping grounds. And it was very much "life after the storm," fresh air and scattered vegetation.

I met Frank's stepson who voluntarily confirmed Frank's standing as a millionaire. But he also confirmed that Frank had accumulated his fortune in a ruthless and, what most people would call, a miserly way. It had endeared him to very few. I had experienced that side of Frank for myself. His own family had barely concealed loathing for him as he had allegedly used the prospect of inheriting his wealth in order to manipulate family members to take positions on matters that they would not ordinarily take. But, it appeared that this strategy had run its course. They had felt so tarnished by following in his footsteps that they seemed to have reached the point of drawing a line in sand and saying, "No further."

One fact that I found interesting was that he was rumoured to have been held in custody for a week in connection with the murder of his wife. At the time it appeared to be just one of those rumours that get hung around people's neck in an attempt to bring them "down to earth." And, in any case, according to the story, he had been released at the end of the week for lack of evidence. But, as I got to know him, and with some hindsight, I realise that, if these allegations were true, they would make sense of his abrupt behaviour that was hard to understand otherwise. For example his apparent wish to fund a religious group while showing no interest in living by spiritual principles. And the alleged threats of cutting anyone out of his inheritance, if they crossed him or got in his way.

Then there was his alleged tendency to manipulate and to control those around him with the prospect of inheriting his wealth. And there was his apparent disregard for any "collateral damage" that might occur as a consequence of his decision-making (as I was about to find out.) But, above all, perhaps there was his spendthrift lifestyle that must have made living with him very difficult for anyone in close proximity, as his wife must have experienced. What was clear

from discussion with his small circle of "friends" in Miami was that he was respected for his
achievement in amassing a fortune, rather than for his virtues as a human being.

I remember there being much hilarity within this group, when I announced that before jetting out to South America I wanted to get my spectacles mended. No one knew what "spectacles" were, let alone where there was a place that would mend them! After a short spell of miming, we eventually established that I was looking for a place that mended "glasses." It was the first time that I realised I was in a foreign culture, even if we have a few words in common.

Now that I knew that there were some very major questions about his past, relations with Frank became a little strained. On the one hand, he had been investigated, and cleared of any wrongdoing. On the other hand, those who knew him best seemed to be highlighting some of his unsavoury behavioural patterns as evidence that he was capable of doing that which he had been accused of! As a yogi, this situation posed several dilemmas for me. I was in no doubt that we all had "pasts," of which we might not be very proud. On the other hand, the path I had chosen to follow involved a process of owning up to things and taking the care not to make the same mistakes again. Frank showed no inclination to own up to previous mistakes of any sort and seemed content to replicate some of his previous "dubious" behaviour. Against this background, the prospect of him founding his own "community" certainly didn't fill me with joy! We had a saying that seemed appropriate in this context. "As the seed, so the tree."

I don't remember much about our flight, or of our arrival in Lima, Peru. This did feel like being a long way from home. There were a few Brits dotted around the place. I met one former British sailor, replete with naval beard, who had jumped ship during the war and who had subsequently decided to settle down in Lima. I didn't see him with a Peruvian partner, but I suspect that that might have been part of the attraction for him. I also met an elderly lady who had come to South America on tour, with a dance troupe, in the 1920s. She did not give a reason for what lay behind her decision to settle down so far from home but I wouldn't have been surprised if romance, likewise, had been a factor.

I don't remember much about Peru, other than it was quite cold, so it must have still been winter there. And there was an oddness of seeing "Kramer v Kramer" advertised outside the local cinema. This was a film that was just breaking at home and somehow it seemed strange that a remote city in South America should be bang up to date with the latest trends. Perhaps, I was just hoping that Lima had escaped the rampant globalisation that had emerged in other corners of the world. But it had not, and probably most Peruvians were very pleased that it hadn't!

After a few days in town to orient ourselves, we discovered a vegetarian restaurant that hosted small talks in a fairly impromptu way. So both Frank and I agreed to do a double bill, with him promoting his new aspirations to start a community down here, followed by me talking about the reasoning behind a yogic lifestyle. We were booked into a better quality of hotel in Lima but, despite my protestations, we were still sharing a room. Although, by now, it was becoming increasingly obvious to both of us that this was not a workable arrangement.

I don't really remember much about the subsequent days, only the day of the presentations, themselves. As planned, Frank went first. To my horror, I realised that he had organised things in his mind in such a way that I was being cast as the founding member of his community. Worse than that was the implication that I was the one who was going to father the vegetarian babies that would form the basis of his "brave new world."

It was clear now that our double act could not continue! He was certainly getting in the way of my work and, by putting me at the centre of his project, he was clearly attempting to build a structure on very sandy soil.

But, what shocked me most about this scenario was that it seemed that he had not heard a word I had said about the reason for me being there. Or, maybe he had heard my words then merely superimposed his own meaning! Whatever, he had hijacked my identity for his own ends and I was not amused by that. Of course, it was important for me to remain calm in this situation.

But, such was the shock of this development that, for the first time, I began to realise that here was a man who seemed capable of anything! In the light of his behaviour in Lima, I started to seriously think that there might be some credence in the rumours that had been circulating in Miami! I wasn't afraid for my safety. What concerned me was that I might have inadvertently become a bit-player in whatever game he might be playing. Anyway, I was next on in the restaurant and I used my allotted time to undo any damage that may have been done by Frank's contribution, without overtly contradicting the contents of his speech. I used the time also to outline some of the principles that formed the basis of yogic life.

There were about twenty people crammed into the smallish room, almost exclusively of women, which raised the question – was spirituality here seen as belonging primarily in the domain of the womenfolk? The audience seemed to react fairly well to my presentation and any harm that may have been done by Frank's talk seemed to have been avoided.

Fig. 2 shows me in the restaurant, mid flow. The photo was taken on a camera that had been kindly presented to me by Frank's circle of friends in Miami, who had been shocked by the prospect of me going into South America without a camera.

If the truth were to be told, I was still feeling more than a little betrayed by Frank's misrepresentation. So, at the end of our talks, when one of audience said there was a small group heading for the mountains the next day, and asked if I'd care to join them, I leapt at the chance to put some cooling off space between my roommate and me.

That evening, as I was pottering around in my hotel room, I received a call from reception informing me that there were three people in reception to see me. I had no idea who might want to meet me, here, in the centre of Lima. The names reception had given me gave no clues except that they suggested that they were all Peruvians. The plot thickened! When I eventually made it down to the spacious reception area I found that I recognised only one of the three faces awaiting me. It looked like what in fact it turned out to be. A young woman, (whom I recognised from the restaurant audience, earlier in the day,) and her middle-aged parents, whom I had not seen before. Curiouser and curiouser!

In keeping with the culture of Peru, it was the father who spoke first, although it was his daughter who translated his quick-fire bursts of animated Spanish, into a vaguely recognisable version of English. (I have to concede though that her English was much more fluent than my Spanish.) It turned out that Mum and Dad had come along because their daughter wanted to surrender her life, in order to become my disciple! This proposition was a non-starter on the grounds that it was a central principle of our yogic life that there were no "gurus" to get in the way of our direct line to the Source!

But, I noticed there was another factor playing a part in my response to the prospect of taking responsibility for this girl's spiritual development. And, that was a concern that I could not accept the responsibility for this girl. It was not that I had any devious plan in mind. Rather it was the prospect of having my head turned inadvertently. It was a charge that was regularly laid at our feet by critics of our lifestyle. "Are you not just running away from the pressures of the modern world?"

Until this point, I had been able to reply, in all honesty, that I had been drawn towards a life enhancing experience and was certainly not running away from anything. I had discovered an experience far more satisfying than anything my past life had to offer, and had been running towards it and not away from anything! But now there certainly was something I felt inclined to run away from and I think I knew then that this yogic lifestyle was unsustainable for me. It was only a matter of time, and of choosing the "right circumstances," to sever my ties.

When it came, about a year later, it was akin to leaving a five-year relationship! But, in that moment, the decision had pretty well been made! It was simply a matter of choosing the circumstances under which the least damage would be likely to ensue. But my yogic routine was to continue pretty much as before for another three years. As mentioned in the second chapter, I was to meditate nearly every day for the next thirty years.

Some people might think it was quite courageous to turn my back on all this and step into the "real world," but as my beloved London teacher would no doubt have pointed out, it would have taken a lot more courage to stay and work these issues through in yoga!
With hindsight I can see now that it was just a "nervous wobble," and that my yogic life was never in any real danger. But at the time, it took on a much more fearsome aspect.

As far as I can remember it took about two hours the next day to reach the mountains, which I was told were fifteen thousand feet tall. I remember meditating at that height and having a very powerful experience. Without a doubt these mountains are a very special place! I hadn't seen Frank that morning, so he was probably wondering where I'd gotten to. It seemed healthy that we should spend some time apart. After all, our arrangement only covered providing assistance for Frank through airports and the like. I was not contracted as his personal butler.

It was early afternoon when we returned to Lima. There was a lot of high spirits in the car on the way back and it was this buzz that I stepped out of the car and made my way up to our room to have some lunch. On entering the room I immediately noticed that all of Frank's possessions had gone. He'd done a bunk, and what's more, he was holding my return ticket to Miami! How was I going to get back to the States now? Yes, I had money in my bank for the trip from the US to London, but not enough to get me back home from South America. Suddenly, Blighty seemed a very long distance away!

I rushed downstairs firstly to check that the room that had been booked in his name had been paid for. It had, mercifully! And secondly, I wanted to find out when he had checked out of the hotel so that I could decide if there was any point in staging a pursuit. I was informed by reception that he had left just after lunchtime, which probably meant that he was about an hour ahead of me. There was still hope of him being in the terminal somewhere! It was certainly true that the strains in our double act were beginning to show, and maybe it was the right time to walk away from it. But I had done nothing, in my opinion, which merited being dumped, unceremoniously at the far side of the world (if you live in the UK) with no return ticket!

I took a taxi to the airport building in the hope that I might still catch him there, though I had not given much thought to what I would say if he was there. When I got inside the terminal building I was immensely relieved to see him still standing in the check-in queue, though from the expression on his face, he was not pleased to see me. It was the look of a cornered animal, now full of anger and contempt. I may have been the bedrock of his community yesterday, but today it seemed that I had become his worst enemy! Seen from my perspective, his grievance appeared fairly irrational. His features had become Golum-like. It became apparent that he demanded total control over my movements, at all times of the day.

Clearly, this was a man who was used to having things his own way! He seemed a little embarrassed at how his speech of the day before had been exposed for what it was, a bundle of distortions! Well, I was not impressed by his alleged wealth, and I certainly had no intention of colluding in his plans to start a community. And I was happy to make this matter clear.

I rummaged through my mind for guidelines as to handle situations like this, where time played a critical part. On the one hand, I wanted to remain peaceful throughout, what was turning into, a difficult situation. And, on the other hand, I wanted to be sure that I used whatever time was left to significantly influence the outcome of this situation! These two considerations were in conflict, so I decided to search my memory banks for some examples of how it was appropriate for a yogi to behave in this sort of situation. The only vaguely similar situation I could think of was when one of my teachers was trying to keep control of a group of over-enthusiastic porters. In the midst of a very busy Indian railway station, they were trundling off in all directions with our luggage. In response to this split-second crisis, she transformed herself in order to take on the mannerisms of a "shakti," or powerhouse. In an instant her strict voice barked out instructions, and the chaotic situation was transformed into a modicum of order!

No sooner had this example come into my head than I felt a surge of power passing through my body. In the midst of a busy International airport, I pointed dramatically at Frank. "That man stole my air tickets!"

The commotion was sufficient to arouse the attention of a local uniformed policeman, whose involvement was in turn sufficient to attract an apparently more senior plain-clothed officer. The plain-clothes policeman got the gist of issue and stepped over to speak to Frank.

"Is it true? Do you have this man's air ticket? Let me see inside your hand luggage." In common with the behaviour of many schoolyard bullies, Frank's face was completely transformed in the presence of a higher authority. He meekly reached inside his jacket. In his hand was the ticket concerned, and, anxious not to stir up more trouble with the police, he surrendered it to the plain-clothes policeman. In turn, the policeman returned it to me with a smile of self-satisfaction that seemed to say that he was pleased at having defused yet another crisis.

Obviously, staying longer in Lima would cost money, and that was something I didn't have a lot of. The sooner I got back in the States, the sooner I could plan my next move. I enquired at the desk if there was another Miami flight due to fly out later that day and, to my immense relief, I discovered that there were vacant seats on a flight later that night. So I took a taxi back to my hotel and hurriedly packed in good time to be back at the airport for the evening flight.

When I got back at the airport I noticed a line of Hispanic speakers standing in the adjacent line. They were visibly distinguishable from the local Peruvians because of their more colourful Caribbean clothing. I wasn't paying a lot of attention to them because I was still monitoring the effects on me of this air ticket business. I was just vaguely aware of their presence a few feet to my right.

Then, suddenly, there was an almighty roar from this line, and they rushed forward through the check-in desk, and straight through a plate glass window, that shattered with an almighty crash. They then ran out onto the runway, which was straight ahead. And with obvious pre-planning, they made their way to the steps leading up to a particular Braniff Airlines plane, and climbed aboard.

The reaction of the security services to this breech was to run gleefully around the terminal weapons at the ready. As I recall, several shots were fired, but with this amount of water under the bridge, I accept that this could be my in my imagination. Anyway, I was trained to deal with this sort of mayhem. Street disturbances and volatile flash mobs were relatively common in India at that time. So it was a scenario for which I was trained. I simply froze, as moving targets are often seen as more of a threat than static ones in panic situations, and I instantly meditated to take me out of body consciousness and to still the mind, and so to go beyond the influence of the chaotic scenes around me.

When, a few minutes later, we boarded our plane there was a nervous buzz as people turned to their neighbour to exchange dramatic stories. The prevailing account was that these had been Cubans, set free from Cuba's jails by Fidel Castro, as a gesture of defiance against the West. Apparently, one hundred of these individuals and their families had been accepted into Peru by the Peruvian government. Only, the one hundred Cubans didn't particularly want to live in Peru, being more attracted by the thriving Hispanic community in Florida. They had made their grievance known by smashing the plate glass window that stood between them and the airfield, and by occupying an empty plane that stood on the tarmac. I never did find out any more about how this matter was resolved but it was another piece of drama, adding a bit more adventure to my trip.

Meanwhile, I recognised that, back in Lima, there was also a young woman who was seeking spiritual guidance ASAP. I phoned London, and suggested that one of the North American teachers get down here soon, and passed on the contact details. I never heard any more about Peruvian developments, (though I heard recently that there is now a thriving centre in Lima.) There were issues about detachment here for me. When I left Peru, I was also stepping out of any responsibility for anything that might, or might not, happen here.

I have only very vague memories of my return to the States. But I do remember returning to Frank's son-in-law's warehouse where I had stored my summer clothes. The son-in-law was horrified to hear about the air ticket incident, but showed no sign of doing anything about it. It was only then that I got that this was an entire family in collusion, focussing on the big prize to be had, his inheritance. I had the feeling that the final irony Frank had in his mind was to generate some kind of "community" based on rules that he would dictate, and then there would be one final contemptuous gesture towards his long-suffering family. He would then channel his money towards this community, leaving his family with nothing! Paradoxically, I think that his family's willingness to tolerate his bad behaviour, in pursuit of the bigger prize, had only diminished them in Frank's eyes. But then I had experienced for myself just how difficult it was to stay in his good books! Whatever, it was with some relief that I walked away from the entire situation.

The question for me was, where to now? In situations like this, I found it advisable to take advice. The advice I'd been given in London, prior to my South American adventure, had been spot-on. So, it was another phone call to London that seemed most appropriate again at this point. I was primarily wanting to find out if there was anything useful I could be doing while over on this side of the Pond. To my delight, my teacher informed me that a centre in Toronto, Canada, was just about to start on a complete paint-job, if I fancied the task. At around the same time, some money arrived in my bank account from my previous employer. So now, not only did I have a reason for going to Toronto, I had the means too!

It was only a few days later that I flew out of the Sunshine State, heading for the cooler climate of Canada. The plane passed through New York and Buffalo on our way north, so I arrived in Canada in an almost deserted plane. From the outset, it was clear that this place was very different to the one I had left. There was almost a European feel to the place. The casual, what appears on the surface to be, "chaos" of America was replaced by a reassuring "European" orderliness! (Of course, the American airport experience has been transformed post 9/11. Now getting to an aircraft resembles passing through an endless military assault course. By boarding time, I am usually willing to trade places with any Islamic militants around and who are willing to forego their eternal place in heaven!)

Anyway, I arrived in late summer when it was still quite hot and over-night in Canada it turned into winter, when seriously thick clothing was necessary. I was quite engrossed in my painting when, about a week later, the call came through inviting me to attend a conference the following week, in New York. It was the senior teacher from London who informed me that NGO status (non-governmental organisation) had recently been requested and granted, by the UN. This was one of their NGO conferences and I was assured that I would know what to say when I got there. The secret, she said, was to stay yog-yukt, connected in yoga.

But before I left Toronto, I managed to fit in a couple of days to familiarise myself with Toronto, and with the Canadian psyche. I had wondered, for a long time, how Canada could be so geographically close to the US, and share so much of their heritage, yet operate economic and cultural models which were so palpably at variance with the models that were operating in the US. I had travelled through countries in the Far East that were more influenced by the US approach to things than its next-door neighbour, Canada. And, Canadians seemed to be proud of that fact!

About four of us made the car journey together, down from Canada to New York. Once again, there was the strange experience of passing through customs, this time from the ordered Canadian side to the much more relaxed, if (apparently) less structured US side. Another contrast struck me as I probed about in my mind yet again, in one final attempt to put my metaphorical finger on just what it was that made these two countries such a contrast. As I have mentioned before, I had immediately been attracted by the "orderliness" of Canada. At the same time, I had some good friends in the US and probably found Americans to be more "fully expressed" than their northern neighbours. Perhaps that's what it was. Perhaps Americans were just as shrewd at selecting "the best way to do things"; it was just that they built into their processes more scope for self-expression.

Apart from juggling with this contrast of cultures, I don't recall much about this journey which probably lasted just a few hours. I don't remember a great deal about my visit to the UN except that there was a long ramp leading down into the bowels of the building where all the work was done. I also remember the sharp drop in temperature inside this air-conditioned building. The conference that I was attending was located in a room the size of a small theatre. The topic was "Non Renewable Resources." The debate was dominated by black African scholars, quoting worthy studies, which had been conducted in their countries.

This really was a test of my yoga, and of my self-belief, for there was a large part of me that thought that I was completely out of my depth, with nothing of real value to add in this context. However, I managed to hold it together. I put forward an idea that had fairly wide acceptance at the time though, perhaps, not so much now that the environmental agenda has changed so much. My case was that this was a moral dilemma, requiring moral solutions. It was not primarily a physical resource problem. My suggestion was that there were adequate resources to go round, and that what was lacking was the moral will to make this happen. But there was a whole industry invested in the idea that this was a resource issue!

The only other thing I remember from my time in New York was the election of Ronald Reagan. I remember thinking, "Come on America, you've got to be having a laugh?" I never did get that particular joke. Just contrast Presidents Reagan and Obama. Quite a gulf in consciousness!
After my New York visit I was finally free to return to my London base. So, I flew out of JFK airport and back to the UK.

A couple of years later, when I was in the process of reintegrating into mainstream society, I attended a residential men's development group, at which I was invited to share with the group some adventure that I'd been on, in the last couple of years. I chose a cut-down version of the adventures listed in this chapter. The reaction of the course facilitator was to wonder what "trip" I was on. I'm not sure he believed me, or maybe he thought I was just trying to attract attention to myself. In any case, I probably haven't given a full account of this since that day.

About a year later, I finally packed up my career as a yogi. With that great teacher hindsight, I can see now that my greatest mistake was to identify exclusively with my "light" side. All doubts, and basically anything else unsavoury, were swept under the carpet, not because I was afraid of them, or deliberately trying to conceal matters. I suppose I just wanted to keep a tidy ship.

But so far, I haven't felt the need to return to a support structure, (though ill-health makes it a more attractive prospect.) Obviously I have revisited this entire chapter many times. And from a strictly intellectual point of view, I still find the existence of a Supreme Being puzzling. But, I can't deny my experience! It seems that there is compelling evidence on both sides of this discussion, though I'm not really one for sitting on the fence! Never a comfortable place to sit for too long. So, it seems to come down to a straight choice. Either living in a degraded world, with anxiety and probably a measure of hopelessness, or to retain a clarity of vision, keep love in the heart, and keep the sights firmly fixed on perfection!

Chapter 4   The Great Thaw

In this chapter I return to the story of my slow recovery in hospital from a serious brain stem stroke. Looking back on it now, I recognise that I wasn't running particularly positive patterns of thought during this stage of my illness. As you will see, I often let go of my learning about "people making the best choices available at the time," except during my sporadic bouts of "torture." If this was a soft-focus afternoon movie, I would have applied my new-found wisdom consistently and things would have come to a happy conclusion.

But it isn't, I didn't, and they haven't, yet. At least, not in the conventional sense, although, the fat lady still hasn't sung. In my defence for running these thought patterns I can only offer mitigating circumstances. I, too, was making the best of a pretty meagre set of options. So there you are, it wasn't really my fault, phew!

I have also included in this chapter some back-story, which would occasionally drift across my consciousness. This is shown in bold type.

Back on the ward, things, at last, started to thaw out. Granted, it was just my right hand, so far, but the rest would surely follow in its own time. It soon became my party piece to squeeze the fingers of my visitors. After the squeeze, the visitor of the day would feign surprise at the firmness of my grip. I knew that it was still pretty weak but that didn't worry me unduly because I was prepared to work hard with my physio, once the thaw was complete. The frame of reference I had in mind was that of Douglas Bader, as portrayed by Kenneth More in the film "Reach For the Sky." I had learned how to channel my mind in my yogic days and so had the ability to remain on target in circumstances that would distract most people (call it the "barking dog" factor.)

There was still no movement yet in the rest of my body, but I confidently expected to be back at work, and fully restored, within six months. This was not just cockiness, but the result of putting together all the pieces of evidence I had gleaned from the nursing staff, and factoring in my capacity to work single-mindedly in pursuit of a goal. Talking of movements, I was beginning to get a bit frustrated with my nurses euphemistically referred to as my "bowel regime." They would crush senna, using their pestles and mortar, then load it in to my feeding tube. I would much rather have been left alone so that I could permanently cut this whole unsavoury episode out of my life. It seemed logical to me that if this senna feed was cut out then this unsavoury episode could be brought to an end. Why they couldn't see this was a mystery. As it was, different nurses would come in the following day and act shocked that I "had a little present" for them. I felt like screaming at them, "Well, I wouldn't if you lot would stop feeding me that senna."

This seemed, at the time, like a major violation. It felt like a massive intrusion, like a co-pilot intervening and taking control of the flight unannounced. Nobody had asked permission or even informed me that this intrusion was going to happen. Presumably, this "regime" had been in place for some time now but I was only waking up to it now. In a rather uncharitable way, it felt a bit like the lunatics had taken over the asylum.

This was the beginning of a whole process that inevitably accompanies disability, and I didn't much like where it was going. If Princess Diana had three people in her marriage then I suddenly found about thirty-three people inside my head. Of course, now I understand, with a more rounded logic, why it was necessary for them to be there, and to do what they did. If I was forced, I could even say I'm grateful for their united effort. But, at the time, it felt like being elbowed aside by strangers in my own living room.

One of the skills I used to teach in businesses was visual acuity, noticing things with peripheral vision, and so, making decisions on the basis of much more complete information. In hospital, I can recall several occasions when I was leaning badly in my bed, usually to my right. A nurse would generally answer my call for help, but then would enquire, "What is the problem?" It was difficult to understand in some instances what part of the problem she couldn't see! Visual acuity was not an area where some parts of the NHS score highly!

Around this time, there was an international rugby match involving Scotland. Against Wales, I think. Pam judged, correctly, that this match was a match which, in normal circumstances, I would not want to miss. However, when she arrived early next day to watch the match and had gone through the laborious process of signing up for pay-as-you-go TV, I found that the winning or losing a rugby match really didn't matter to me. It occurred to me much later that there must have been many mortally injured men and women lying on the battlefield, for whom, the outcome of their particular battle had ceased to matter.

Such were my concentration levels that I had no sense of the pattern of the play. There seemed to be some brightly coloured dots running around on the screen. And, of course the dots appeared to me to be in duplicate. In fact, there even appeared to be two TV screens and as much as two yards apart at that! There was too much information for me to process and there was an overwhelming sense of nausea as it began to be clear to me that I was about to re-engage, from a much weakened position, with a world that was becoming increasingly complex. I really couldn't find the strength to sit through this ordeal. So I asked to lie down flat again.

I recognise now that Pam may have been disappointed if she was looking for signs of normality from that day's events. She certainly didn't get them, what with my apparent indifference and general lack of enthusiasm.

In many ways I recognised that this whole ordeal must have been just as hard for her. At critical points I had lost consciousness. But she had been left to worry about the outcome.

And then there was the pressure of every day life. From our conversations, I gathered that a vast array of different agencies must have been beating a pathway to her door in search of answers she couldn't possibly give. It was a source of great sadness to me that I was in no position to "protect" her from all that. In reality, of course, it would probably have been her protecting me but such harsh truths were not allowed to spoil my illusions!

The next stage of the thaw occurred when my right arm began to move. It wasn't much of a thaw, initially. Just a few inches of movement to begin with. But it was what seemed, at the time, to be the start of an inexorable process, even though it might take a few months for the thaw to be complete and for the muscles to build up strength again. My strength seemed to have been significantly affected during my illness, and by a long spell in this bed. It had still not occurred to me, at this stage, that this loss of power from my limbs might be a long-term state of affairs. Over the space of about a week my arm finally made it to my mouth. At last, I was able to wipe the excess saliva that drained continuously from my mouth. But not yet, deal with that blocked nostril, or with the scalp I so badly wanted to scratch!

It is difficult to be taken seriously when there is saliva constantly leaking from your mouth. (Not that I wanted, very often, to be taken seriously. I was busy giggling and building relationships at every opportunity.) The ability to raise my hand had far-reaching implications that I did not fully understand at the time. It meant that I could be independent at mealtimes, feeding myself. Assuming, of course, that they were ever going to allow me to eat! I took it as a personal slight that they persisted with this notion that I could not eat, leaving me vulnerable to these dreaded attacks. On a couple of occasions, I even summoned the swallowing specialist adamant that this ban on eating was a mistake. Maybe other patients with this condition had swallowing problems but I could look back on a lifetime of successful swallowing. I had the identity of a "swallower" so when some authority figure, who I had never met before, came along and told me I wasn't allowed to eat, I wasn't very happy. When, subsequently, the swallowing specialist gave me a mouthful of yoghurt to swallow; amazingly it just sat in my mouth. However, my identity as a "swallower" was never in any doubt at this stage and I reasoned instead that there must have been some environmental factor at work, causing this very odd response. Perhaps it was just that it is difficult to swallow on demand. After all I didn't normally involve my conscious mind in the act of swallowing. I left it to my unconscious mind. Maybe my unconscious mind just didn't like being bossed by my conscious mind? Who knows?

One thing was clear. I couldn't expect to be to be taken seriously in my campaign to be given food to eat, until such time as I got my act together. I was very disappointed with my performance at these sessions. I had a lifetime of experience that I could point to as evidence that I was perfectly capable of both chewing and swallowing my food, yet for some strange reason I wasn't able to demonstrate it when it really mattered. I had the "identity" but not for some reason, the "competence" to demonstrate the skill when it really mattered.

It was to be one of my greatest frustrations over the months ahead that, from now on, different areas of my life were to be policed by different agencies. Not just temporarily but, it appeared, into the long-term future. A future that was completely unpredictable, as there were unexpected twists and turns on this strange road on which I was now travelling. My private world had been carved up so that decisions about what I could and could not eat and drink, and how much of each, now lay in the hands of "dieticians" and "speech and language therapists." Decisions about the timing and structure of my "bowel regime" lay in the hands of the nursing staff. Decisions about the content of my daily medications were taken, behind the scenes, by a team of ward doctors. Decisions about which muscle groups to exercise, and by how much, were taken by physiotherapists.

I may have just taken my eye off the highway for a short while but now a "monstrous regiment" of professionals had moved in and taken over the steering wheel. Although all of the individuals concerned had been very respectful, in some cases even charming, it was beginning to feel a bit crowded in the control room. Here I was, aged 52, and with no current job, and redundant even in the context of the key decisions affecting this body, or what was left of it.

It was around this time that the conspirators made their most audacious move to date. They followed me onto a train. There were five of them, the usual suspects. They surrounded me with the usual intimidation, and forced me out of the train and across a bridge, onto the platform opposite. Eventually, we boarded a train headed back into town, getting out at a large building belonging to Edinburgh University. It soon became clear that they wanted to keep me in this place. Now there was a Parisian food supplier who fed me, remotely, using daily phone calls to trigger my feeding. With horror, I realised that the Parisian supplier would not be able to locate me in this building, and so would not be able to trigger my remote feeding. There was a feeling of genuine terror as I began to grasp that with each passing day, I would get weaker and so, more susceptible in their hands. Any escape plan would have to be carried out before I lost any more strength.

But surely Pam would notice my absence? She had proved very effective in tracking me down, no matter where in the hospital I'd been sent. Even when I was farmed out to a remote rural branch she had somehow tracked me down. But surely, not even Pam would find me here. No, I had to rely on my own resources if I was going to get out of this one. I was aware that my legs weren't working but I reasoned that they would kick in, much the same as would a car that needed a jump-start. All that was needed was to build up sufficient momentum. And, it was this technique that I used to escape after three days in this building. I ran, first, along a lengthy corridor. Then I was out into the Queen's Park. And sure enough, my trusty legs did what they had to do in order to get me out of danger.

I took the earliest opportunity, on my return to hospital, (don't ask me how I got there,) to check out whether Pam had noticed my absence over these three traumatic days. I was a bit taken aback when she said that she'd been visiting me in the hospital for the last three days, did I not remember? For the first time, I began to suspect that there might be a recurring pattern to all these adventures, though I was not yet ready to dismiss them as "neurotic episodes." Events were still so "real" that I had no reason yet to doubt them.

Another thing I noticed about hospital life was that when I buzzed, my call, as you would expect, was answered quite quickly. Nurses would march into my room, switch off my "call-waiting" sign, and then march back out, with the promise to "be back in a minute." But I don't remember this promise ever being met. It actually got to the point that whenever I used to hear these fateful words, "I'll be back in a minute," I used to reply, inside my head, "Oh no you won't!" My best opportunity to get my needs met came when, a nurse with a willingness to communicate would come into my room with the intention of running through this nursing ritual. I would ignore their protests about "having something else to do" and would instead mime out a representation of whatever it was I wanted. Usually I could get my needs met using this method. Was it a bit manipulative? Maybe, but the nurses were being a bit manipulative in the first place. Anyway, I was primarily concerned with strategies that would enable me to stay alive in, what I experienced to be, a fairly hostile environment. With the benefit of hindsight, I suspect that the ward may have been trying to meet a management target here in respect of the length of time which nurses took to answer buzzers.

On one occasion, a nightshift nurse swept into my room and put on the light, asking in a rushed voice, "What it was that I wanted." When I replied, unintelligibly, to her question she turned abruptly on her heels and marched back out saying, "If you don't tell me what you want, I can't help you." And with that, the light went off and the door was pulled to. In the darkness it felt very frustrating to be back at the end of the queue, where I initially started. And what made it worse, was the realisation that I probably had been characterised as a "time waster" and as someone who was just "acting up." This, almost certainly, would mean that my call would be attributed a low priority and it would be some time before a second nurse would appear. This, presumably, was not considered to be part of the target, if there was one in the first place.

The hardest part of this whole business to take was the recurring sense of injustice. The nursing staff would attribute their own theory of causality, a theory taken from their own world and projected onto me.

In my private world, I got used to running videos of previous funny scenes or tapes of funny lines from the past much in the way that Brian Keenan had projected movies onto his wall. I would often giggle at a memory of a funny incident that was passing through my mind. Invariably, this laughter would be interpreted as being some kind of commentary about something that was going down in the room. This mistaken belief would then shape their subsequent orientation to me, good or bad. One nurse accused me of something, then said not to deny it because she had seen me doing whatever it was. Now I can't remember what it was that I had been accused of doing. But I am sure that, whatever it was that the nurse thought she saw me doing, it was no more than a piece of behaviour taken out of context and reframed by the nurse to give it some meaning which was not present in the original piece of behaviour.

It was a pattern I was to grow used to, and one that gave a whole new meaning to the expression "being framed." Any subsequent laughter, which would often accompany my sense of disease at finding myself in the centre of yet another drama was interpreted as "guilty laughter" and merely confirmed them in their verdict. And often there was a "scatter gun" approach taken. "And if he's not guilty this time then I'm sure he must have done it at other times. So, anyway here's a bullet!" I am not suggesting that my behaviour was always blameless. It wasn't. But generally, I was willing to live with the consequences of my actions. Just not with the consequences of actions that had been wrongly laid at my doorstep. Even my beloved physios reckoned towards the end of my stay with them that my continuous giggling must be down to the fact that I had a soft spot for one of their number. A belief lifted straight out of their world and placed at my feet. It was true that I felt great affection for all the physios, and for all those others who went that extra mile to help lift me out of the crevasse that I seemed, inadvertently, to have stumbled into. But the physios stood out from the rest because all the way though this long ordeal they had related to me in terms of my potential for recovery, and not just as the beached whale, which I think some of the others tended to see.

I was reminded of an earlier experience that I had had many years previously in London. I was travelling along the road on my motor bike when an Irish lady stepped off the pavement and onto the road directly in front of me. In order to avoid mowing her down, I steered my bike into the edge of the pavement and opted for a tumble over my handlebars. I was lying prone on the pavement when the little Irish lady approached me. She was effusive in her praise. "God bless you, you saved my life," and more lines like this, which suggested that she realised how close she had come to a sticky end. A few minutes later, as I was being loaded into the back of an ambulance, I was amazed to hear the same Irish lady pontificating with a small bunch of onlookers. She had seen my L plate, so maybe, she thought, the accident had been caused by my inexperience as a driver? This explanation seemed to fit the facts and there were nods of agreement from the group.

This was revisionism in my own lifetime, and now, here again it was going down in hospital! It was all happening again! Blatant falsehoods were being perpetrated with inconvenient facts being overlooked on an almost daily basis. Neutral parties would just fall in with the explanations that seemed most likely to fit the truth, irrespective of any evidence that might point in other directions. And, although, generally, these were to do with matters of little consequence, collectively they did start to add up. It felt a bit like ritualised abuse.

I was reminded of some childhood exchanges with my uncle, a former heavyweight boxing champion. He would show his affection by planting his clenched fist in my face and saying, "That's what you get for nothing, a bunch of fives. See what you get for something!" I think I was given the same message by some of the ward "heavyweights." If, subsequently, I have appeared a bit touchy about false allegations, then this is the reason. Remember, my orientation at the time was to continue down the highway. I firmly believed that this detour would turn out to be no more than yet another adventure, in a life already rich with them.

But I finally worked out how to overcome this forced-feeding issue, and thus, break free from my torturers. The answer had been in front of me all the time. I had just failed to realise it. The staff had clearly overlooked the fact that I was getting fed via a remote control telephone link to a Paris-based firm. So there was no need for tube feeding to continue.

A part of me was astonished that no one had spotted this duplication before. But, at last it had been discovered. A veritable "get-out-of-jail" card! So, it was with considerable excitement that I shared this development with Pam who rapidly dismissed it with her usual bluntness.

"Nonsense Stuart, you are not fed from Paris!" It was like a hot sun burning through a morning cloud. The belief, which had seemed so certain just a few minutes ago, now evaporated before my eyes. The only mystery now was how I had come to believe it in the first place. I was usually quite discerning about what I would and would not believe, (no doubt some would take issue with this, given the evidence of the last chapter,) so it seemed odd that I had been careless enough to allow this unsubstantiated belief into my head.

My right leg was the next limb to take advantage of the thaw. As with my arm, there was very little strength left in this limb. I wasn't even able to move it under the weight of the bedclothes. The physios wasted no time in catching wind of this partial "thaw out." They would appear first thing every weekday and ask if I wanted to do physiotherapy. I never missed a session, even on a Monday, when sometimes I had not slept a wink over the weekend. They seemed to be the only ones who saw me in terms of my potential, and who were focussed on bringing this out. For my part, I wanted to get back to being me, and was prepared to make whatever effort was required.

The physios were my big hope and I had great respect for all of them, although my frequent giggling fits probably didn't convey this. At the time, I was under the impression that I controlled my laughter, but with hindsight I was probably under its control. I had certainly started the ball rolling by my conscious decision to lighten up. But somewhere along the line my laughter had got out of my control. As the physio in my rehab hospital pointed out, I would break into laughter at the very point when my limb extension was getting painful. Initially at least, this was very confusing feedback for my therapists, who tended to be horrified once they cracked this code. I have subsequently met other individuals who show signs of emotional lability. In some cases, it took the form of compulsive crying. With hindsight, I am glad that I had opted for the laughter route.

Previously, I had grasped the thorny nettle by running laughter workshops in businesses, alongside other more conventional courses. During these workshops, I would suggest that when we laugh endorphins are released into our bodies, regardless if our reason for laughing was genuine in the first place. Most people probably consider that it would be a sign of madness if they were to laugh

without a very appropriate reason, like a joke, or a funny situation. In this way, they travel through life hopeful that they will come across something that will "make them laugh." Or, in more formal language, a stimulus that would justify their response and make it seem appropriate, in their eyes. Needless to say, in today's world, these opportunities to laugh don't come along as regularly as we might wish so we pump a good deal less endorphins through our bodies than we might. The cost of this is a lot more stress in our lives than would be necessary if we just learned to laugh for laughter's sake.

I remember, in particular, working with one group of civil servants in this area. While they didn't voice any opposition to the main thrust of the argument, it was clear from the furtive looks they shot at each other, that they felt that stoicism would be a much more appropriate response to the circumstances prevailing in their office! Yes, I know I'm not in any position to give health lectures any more. I accept that my credibility is pretty much shot through. However, the same logic shines through, to me at least. I certainly wouldn't recommend some of my more recent health decisions!

Weekends tended to drag, as the physios were not in. It felt like being in a boarding school over a public holiday when all your playmates had gone home. It was simply a question of treading water until the physios reappeared on Monday morning. Everything they touched seemed to add quality. They alone seemed to know how to position me comfortably in my bed. It was them who introduced me to the idea that I could take limited control of my own position in the bed. And so, by managing the bed's remote control for myself, I could select a position that would offer a means of allowing me to change to a more comfortable position. I couldn't understand why this was not promoted by the nursing staff, as this would get me more off their backs. And probably, most importantly, the physios introduced me to the art of walking my fingers along surfaces, and so significantly increasing my range of movement. Oddly enough, years later, my current physio is working hard to eradicate this "lazy" way of moving my right arm, and using instead my biceps.

My body felt as though it was surrounded by a magnetic field. For some reason, I found it almost impossible to move my arms away from my body. The sensation at the time was that they were magnetised to my body and that an invisible force field was operating all around me. I was hoping that, in the fullness of time, physiotherapy would help me to overcome this restriction. From my perspective as a patient, it seemed odd that the physiotherapy service should not be available for two out of every seven days. (I realise that the physios themselves might have a different perspective, and there is likely to have been a long history of political wrangling on this matter, with valid arguments, both for and against.) But when the physios left the building the hospital lost a great deal of its therapeutic edge and became more of a "hostel."

It was the physios who introduced me to the delights of the "tilt table," a complicated process, involving large wooden tables and lots of heavy-duty leather straps. The end result is that a wooden base slowly rises off a bench pushing the torso into a standing position, secured by leather straps. Most impressive of all was the fact that the elevation of the base was electronically controlled, and what's more, the physios handed the remote to me! For the first time in months I was able to raise myself to a standing position, and stay there!

I remember, from my story about my escape from that Edinburgh University building, that the hardest part of the whole adventure had been that initial movement up and out of my bed. It is difficult to exaggerate the psychological impact of being upright again. It was like revisiting my old self. The amount of additional information that is available from a standing position is immense, but not only that, the viewpoint is much more rounded, enabling a much more complete picture of how events are related. I'd got used to just seeing things from the very limited perspective of my pillow! It was probably lying in bed in this prone position 24/7 that was responsible for my perception that the world revolved around me. I didn't get to see how actions fitted in to a broader framework of causes and reactions, only the little bit of action, the thin slice that was in front of my nose!

It was about this time that the nude ballet dancer appeared. Strictly speaking, this is not a funny story since it involves the dignity of someone's partner, or mother, or grandmother. But I did find it funny, at the time. There were to be many amusing scenarios along the way, each sadly, involving people for whom this was a living nightmare, yet who were unintentional actors in pretty weird situations, nevertheless. In telling these stories it is not that I fail to see the tragedy that lies behind each one. But, seen from another angle, some pretty funny scenarios transpired! And, as they say in hospital wards up and own the country, "You've got to laugh!"

It was in the middle of the night when most patients were fast asleep. As usual, I was lying, hoping to drift off. It was not uncommon for me to remain awake all night, but it never occurred to me that I might have a sleep problem because it was not a characteristic that, historically, I had. It did not form a part of who I believed I was. It was not uncommon for me to lie awake for two or three nights in a row. Many of these would involve horrific scenes so I was usually just glad to make it through to the next morning! Staying alive, throughout all these ordeals was much more important to me than losing a few nights' sleep.

Suddenly an elderly lady, of about eighty, came waltzing down the corridor, her arms swinging about in balletic fashion. Her body was completely naked, but from the smile on her face, it was as though she was living out some old memory. It never occurred to me that she might be experiencing delusions similar to mine because I was utterly convinced that what I had experienced was real and therefore bore no relation to the fantasies of an old lady! This tale may have all the hallmarks of being yet another of my imaginings. However, there is one factor that sets it apart from my other fantasies. When the nightshift came on the following night they were all chortling about his story.

This was referred to as an "acute stroke" ward. So whatever was meant by this term "acute stroke," it seemed capable of sending old ladies over the edge. Or, perhaps it was the drugs they used to treat this illness. (I still had no idea what this term "stroke" actually meant. And, at this stage, perhaps even more curiously, I still had no interest in finding out.)

What puzzles many of the friends who only knew me as a relatively sharp-suited businessman (or, more precisely, a bright-socked businessman) is how, and why, I made the long journey back into the world of commerce. The answer to the "how" part, is that it was largely accidental, if you believe in accidents! When I returned to my home city of Edinburgh, I was lucky enough (if you believe in luck) to get a local government job in training. As a result, I was to get eight year's exposure to training issues, at all organisational levels, and in different organisational settings. As with so many other twists and turns, it was never a deliberate career choice. I suppose there were quite a few transferable skills that I brought with me back from Indian adventures. To help you make sense of this move I've set out some of the transferable skills below.

First, there was an understanding of how, apparently unrelated issues are interconnected below the surface. So, before long, I learned that a "systemic" approach to managing people was more effective (in my opinion) than simply rolling out "the next big idea," which had been our approach in the past. Generally, there was nothing wrong with the "next big idea" itself, we just never really considered that its introduction would inevitably set off a chain

reaction, and that would itself need managing! Little wonder that
workers become sceptical about change!
And then there was my experience of talking in front of large
groups of people and of being able to know which levers needed to
be pulled for significant transformation to occur.

Next, there was my awareness of the importance of "thought
management." In Western business, there is a tendency to over-
look the role of the mind and to assume that, if we create business opportunities, people will automatically step into them.
"Performance coaching" is something that we expect to see on a
Saturday afternoon at the local football ground. But, in a business environment?

After all, people are motivated by earning money aren't they? I
came across quite a few managers who seemed to believe they are.
Well actually no, usually not.

And the proof? If there weren't other factors at play, (both
carrots and sticks) I suppose we would all be drug dealers! But
aren't there some people who have made exactly this choice? Yes,
which just goes to show that there are a few people out there
who are motivated just by earning money. People who are capable
of doing whatever it takes to acquire money, lots of money. But
evidence suggests that they are only a very small minority.

One man famously described me as a "snake-oil salesman." And,
of course, he was right in the sense that my fundamental orientation was to "oil" the wheels of communication in the belief that all
would appear reasonable if those concerned just learned to "hear"
better, what was being said by the different parties.

Of course some managers would run a million miles when confront-
ed with anything that sniffed at all "new agey." Which was entirely understandable. So it was usually necessary to set out the

case along more conventional business lines. I spent many an hour rummaging through garbage, because that's where my client believed that was where his/her truth was to be found.

With hindsight, my one major regret is that I was maybe exploited a bit and "used" by a few unscrupulous employers to promote policies that were (in my judgement) fundamentally unreasonable. Work, for the big banks, for example, or for certain utility companies, where it was clear that corporate bullying was the key driver for improved economic performance.

It was odd, being invited into a company's front room for a few days, only to find that there was something that was obviously shaping events, yet which wasn't being spoken about, (in public at least!) And companies were often quite prescriptive about which topics they were, and weren't, prepared to open up. The more obvious the signs that abuse was taking place, the firmer would be the grip on the training agenda.

One thing that had puzzled me was that I kept wakening up in different wards, or in some cases, different geographical locations. Yet I had no memory of being moved. This was odd! I assumed they must be moving me at night, but one deficiency in this theory was that I was a notoriously light sleeper. Surely I would have woken at least once during transportation?

Fortunately, I was able to clear up this mystery. The construction of the hospital was such that rooms could simply be slid out from their existing location and slotted in elsewhere in the hospital. This also explained how in at least one other ward I had previously seen my greetings cards, (that, incidentally, meant a lot to me, you know who you are,) mounted on the wall. I had made a mental note that, when the time came to leave hospital, I would remember to take with me both sets of cards.

One day a strange lady walked into my room and started to talk about communication aids. From what I could gather, which wasn't much at the time, she was from a private company. It was strange because although I had lost my voice temporarily, I was fully expecting to get it back. I certainly didn't, as yet, have the identity of a "non-speaker."

It seemed to me, that it would be a much better use of scarce resources, if the emphasis in Speech and Language Therapy was laid on therapy that was designed to restore my voice, rather than on wasting time and money on plastic toys. They struck me as a total irrelevance. She said she was from, what sounded like, a dot-com business to me. It seemed as though someone had been briefing a private company about my communication needs! But what I was most, frankly, insulted by in all this was her apparent misdiagnosis of my situation. I still had the identity of "a speaker," in the same way that I had the identity of being "a swallower." She seemed to misunderstand that I was the same fairly well-educated person inside, and that pushing a large button to signal the word "yes" was way below my actual level of competence.

Of course with hindsight I can see that her actions were entirely appropriate to my level of need but my sense of "self" had not adapted sufficiently at the time, and it seemed like a farcical misjudgement of my capabilities. She also gave me a page of letters that was based on the principle that the most commonly used letters appeared on the page first. The theory was that I was to wait for the appropriate letter to be read out, and then I was to press my buzzer to indicate that the correct letter had been reached. A combination of my muscular weakness and Pam's speed of delivery meant that the buzzer rarely sounded at the correct letter, making the task of communicating more difficult not less difficult. Another problem was that, unlike the alphabet, there was no warning that the correct letter was coming up. It was the first of many subsequent discoveries that, what seemed like a good idea on paper, brought with it a set of consequences that, in some cases, were completely unanticipated.

I was in "let's try it" territory for the first time and that was, much later, to extend to the purchase and immediate discarding of several items which, on the surface, held the promise of some benefit.

Probably it appeared to others as rather whimsical. But I was in a completely new situation and experimenting was the only way forward.

With the arrival of British summer time and the arrival of early morning daylight, my mind started to turn its attention to holidays.

There are a series of day trips that I can remember. The first involved a sail in a steamship through the Trossachs. The event passed uneventfully, except that I noticed one of the conspirators disembarking at the same time as me. I remember making a mental note not to be off my guard even on these trips. It seemed that wherever I went, they were only a few steps behind.

Another trip was to a place quite close to Callander. There was a stage full of frozen people that just stood stock still. Together like that, they formed an eerie ensemble, but one which was interesting because it was proof that there were other silent people out there, if only in silent "freak shows!"

The third trip was to Strathpeffer, a place in Rossshire, in the Scottish Highlands, where we had lived for eight years. I remember being in the village square. To my surprise, the road had been dug out and replaced by water, in which sat big sailing ships, which was odd, because Strathpeffer is about 8 miles from the sea. Where there are now hotels, there was a large museum/shop and there were many staff from one of the big hotels, wearing neat uniforms and handing out newspapers and drinks. I had the impression that all of this was set in times gone by. I remember looking over at our previous house and wondering if the present owners would mind letting us look round. There were several stories that took place in this setting, but I remember them only in flashes.

However absurd they seem now, these experiences felt very real at the time.

Of much more value than the yellow buzzer and the page of letters, listed by frequency of use, was an alphabet that had been devised by a former patient who, anecdotally, had been mentioned many times before, and who apparently had had "the same kind of stroke." It was vaguely exciting to think that it wasn't just a common garden stroke but a special "kind" of stroke that I had had, and, apparently, it was quite an uncommon variety!

Imagine my surprise when this trailblazer and his wife suddenly appeared at the door of my room. I became like one of these dogs that squeal with excitement and shake their tales uncontrollably when their owner comes home. Only in my case, I squealed and burst out crying uncontrollably. This was not the sort of welcome I had planned. Seeing him walking into the room was a great boost to my own expectations of recovery. But his speech was a bit more slurred than I had expected from what the nurses had led me to believe when they told me that he had recovered his voice.

Above all, I saw in Alan a template for my own recovery. I really didn't know how this story was going to end, and in Alan's experience, I saw a clear outline of how it could be.

I was also impressed that they had both returned to the ward. Wild horses wouldn't drag me back to this place, once I escaped its clutches.

During our short conversation, Alan briefed me on which hospital I should aim for to get rehabilitation, and gave the name of a good consultant I should seek out. But, perhaps the most significant development was that his wife promised to return for an hour to bring in some of Alan's hospital tools.

And true to her word she turned up with Alan's toys. Most importantly, she brought an alphabet board, set out in QWERTY format, with
punctuation options, and a ""new sentence" option. And it was easy to
use because it had been designed by a user. There was also a pointer
to point at letters, and thus, to create words. At long last, Pam and I
could have a discussion that wasn't just in banner headlines. Though it
was still in opening-paragraph bold type.

Pam arrived while this woman was still in the room. Overhearing the
end of our discussion about the new alphabet, Pam, not unnaturally,
concluded that she must be a speech and language therapist. Imagine
her surprise then when the woman said she knew how hard it must be
to just lie there for months. She went on to say that there had "even
been times when she had crawled onto Alan's bed to give him a hug"
when he was particularly low. Pam listened in amazement, and wondered inside about the extent to which the NHS was breaking out of
its traditional tight-laced-ness to embrace a more holistic approach to
caring for its patients.

It only took a couple of minutes to put her straight on that one.

One day, as I was standing via the tilt table, a doctor poked his head
through the doorway, and said, "That's you, Mr Hepburn, booked in to
have your peg fitted next Wednesday."

It was with some surprise that I received this news. No one had mentioned that there was a problem with my leg, although my left leg had
not even begun to "thaw out." Nor was there any pain in my leg. Nevertheless, in present circumstances, it seemed wisest to follow medical advice so if they thought it best to fit a peg then it was advice I
was prepared to follow. It seemed that only a part of me was going to
come out the other side of this adventure alive.

I decided to adopt the same attitude as Brendan Behan's tramp. I
knew already that they had plans to replace my frozen left arm. It

didn't matter how many parts weren't working, I would just suck in my breath and keep going. Despite framing it in this way, the development continued to churn in my mind. It struck me as odd that the only examples of a peg leg I had seen were both in films, "Treasure Island" and "Peter Pan." When the big day arrived, I remember that a trainee nurse was sent to observe the op as she hadn't seen this done before.

The op was to take place in another, nearby, hospital. It was connected to my present hospital by a long underground tunnel which meant that we began the long journey by descending into the bowels of the hospital, into a very interesting zone, a sort of "underworld." In one room we passed there were a group of doctors playing jazz. Outside the room, there was a large poster pinned to the wall advertising for a jazz singer to join the band. I stopped the trolley long enough to put Pam's name forward because I knew she had been a professional singer, and had trained in jazz singing. It would be a good diversion from all this stress. I later heard that the audition had gone well and that Pam had since joined the band.

Our journey along the tunnel continued.

I woke up back in my room and, to my surprise, saw that both my legs were still there. What had changed however was that there was a tube sticking out of my stomach, capped. On enquiring about this, the nurses informed me that this was my new PEG feeding tube. It was with some relief that I finally understood that the fitting of a Peg related to the fitting of a feeding tube and had nothing to do with my leg.

However, the mental resolve to keep moving forward, regardless of how dark it got on the path, was destined to prove very useful in the years ahead. It reminded me of a forward's rush in the game of rugby. No matter how much battering there was, and which bits of my anatomy were ripped off, the task was to keep heading for the try line.

Eyes closed, and teeth gritted. Ok, ok, maybe there were times during my rugby career when I didn't always practice this as much as I remember doing so.

I discovered that the ward down below was a safe place to overnight. There was a very good charge nurse who understood how to prepare her patients for a good night's sleep. I always slept well here, that is, until one of the conspirators moved in to a room directly across the ward. Worryingly, I saw the rest of the gang arrive to visit him. I noticed that he was now operating under the name "Willie," a change from what he had been called before. I also saw two of the ward cleaners visit him frequently, so regularly in fact, that I got the impression that at least one of them must be close family. This meant that he had agents on the ward that would probably do his bidding. And these cleaners had access to all the rooms! Mmm. The main conspirators never started any trouble in this ward, but their menacing presence made this a less safe place than it had been.

Another strange lady arrived, this time to talk about wheelchairs. I remember thinking that she must be confusing me with someone who used a wheelchair. She went about her work with some earnestness, her measuring tape constantly moving, with references to wheelchair parts that meant nothing to me. I'm glad one of us knew what they were talking about, because I hadn't a clue. I was fortunate enough to have never been in close contact with a wheelchair, and they did not feature in my plans for the future. However, if it gave this lady something to do, and it made her feel valuable in the community, I was prepared to go along with her ideas.

The wheelchair was delivered about a week later, a remarkable turn around, as I have since discovered. It was parked in the corridor outside. To begin with, it appeared to be a rather alien looking object which held no attraction for me in the least. But then I got that it was a way of seeing things beyond the confines of my room. So gradually, I grew to like it. The only problem was that I could only tolerate about an hour in the seat before it became remarkably uncomfortable.

It was usually the physios who would sweet-talk me into the chair, then, (I think deliberately, because they were a crafty bunch,) they would march off at the end of the session, leaving me high and dry. I spent many hours in complete agony, waiting for two nurses to become free to do the transfer back into my bed. But, after a short spell in bed, I would yearn to be back in the chair.

The ability to see things from a different angle was rapidly becoming my overwhelming consideration. Even if it almost always ended badly, with agonising waits. Thus, bit by bit, the wheelchair became part of my identity. And now, a couple of years down the line, it has become almost an extension of my personality.

As I mentioned previously, I had actually done some consultancy work in the NHS. In addition, I also used to work one-to-one with some patients who had been referred to me by their GPs. These patients displayed symptoms that could be as diverse as those of depression and Asperger's Syndrome. They would send them to me for a brief exploration of how their minds were "set up" to cope with the particular circumstances that each was having to cope with. This was seen by some GPs as a valid alternative, or complement, to drug therapy. I certainly learned a lot from it, and hope that I was able to make a difference for some people!

So, I was not entirely new to some of the issues that were prevalent in the NHS, though I wouldn't reveal anything learned then, in this book. You could say that I was watching them, even as they were watching me! And, in a strange sort of way, I was given two years' privileged access to the soft underbelly of the NHS, something of a dubious pleasure! So, those who know me through business will recognise that, throughout, I was trying to come to grips with the nature of the beast that had me firmly in its hand, and which, to my distorted way of thinking, looked ready to devour me.

I think in this next story there is a mixture of the real and the fantasy, but I'm not sure where the one carries forth, into the other. My bed was being pushed somewhere, perhaps for an x-ray. Anyway, we were parked up in a corridor, waiting for some appointment.

The walls were made of clear plate glass windows that allowed me to see through to what looked like giant fish tanks which, rather surprisingly, contained people with no diving gear. On the side that I was attending to there was a typical scene from "The Godfather," a man and woman sitting round a café table with a dodgy looking character sitting in the background. Much to my surprise, the dodgy character got up and approached the couple with a completely calm exterior. When he was just about three feet away from me he calmly stretched over and slit the seated man's throat. Blood spurted everywhere and it was such a complete shock that it set my heart rate shooting up. As a consequence, the heart monitor that was still attached to me started to beep, or buzz, whatever it does.

The nearest doctor came rushing to the scene and shouted the equivalent of "He's crashing!" There followed an almighty doctoral scrum, in the belief that my heart rate was abnormally fast. I remember thinking that their heart rates would have increased too, if they had witnessed what I had just seen.

I found it strange that they did not see the aftermath of the murder that was just two feet in front of them. Surely it was obvious what had increased my heartbeat?

My hand movement at last increased to allow me, with the head slightly bent forward, to scratch the sides of my head, if not as yet, the top of my head. Another benefit was that I was finally able to reach up far enough to unblock my nose. "Managing stasis" was the polite expression that my doctor used to describe this process. In my own little room, and with minimal contact with the nurses, yes, there was plenty of time for "managing my stasis."

However, there was one aspect of this management process that I hadn't anticipated. Just wait for an appropriate "stasis management" moment, then try clearing the left nostril with the right hand. Go on, I dare you!

Obviously, more thought would have to go into devising a new strategy for these changed circumstances.

I wonder if "stasis management" will ever make it to onto the agenda for speed-dating couples? "So, tell me about your stasis management?"

My very last fantasy occurred about two weeks before I left that hospital and the acute part of my health journey, which, in total had lasted three months. Thank God, "And I mean that most sincerely, folks."

There were three of us, and for some reason we thought it appropriate to enter a house that belonged to a family of disembodied spirits. As I recall, we were just curious to know about their living arrangements.

Someone suddenly said that they were on their way back, so we should make a quick exit. While the others made a quick exit via the front door, I suddenly became aware that I could not move from this prone position. As you can imagine, I was filled with horror at the prospect of being discovered in this state, especially as I had no right to be there in the first place.

I think the terror of this situation must have awoken me because the tale ends abruptly at that point. And there was to be no more of these "fantasies" in that hospital, or indeed, in the next one.

Surprisingly, the physios let me down just at the end of my stay. For some reason, they were determined to get me self-propelling in my wheelchair. To this end, they would jam my curled left hand down on the left wheel in a very painful way, and ask me to propel the chair forward.

Needless to say, my left arm just hung there and there was only three or four inches of movement, at each attempt, from my right arm. It became obvious to all parties that a dead horse was being flogged. But they're a persistent lot, these physios. And it became a daily ritual that the dead horse was ritually flogged!

One morning, in swept the consultant, followed by a gaggle of junior doctors. Looking through my file he said, "Well, I don't have any fixed views on what comes next, Mr. Hepburn. It's really up to you. Do you want to stay with us in this hospital, or go on to a specialist rehab unit?"

In just a few seconds I realised that this was the exit I'd been waiting for and, with indecent haste, I indicated as clearly as the remnants of my voice would let me, "The rehab unit!" The consultant smiled, and turning to the other doctors, he said, "Well, we won't take it personally." And, turning to his nominated "scribe," he went on, "And, make a note to contact Dr X at the rehab unit and ask him to drop by and assess Mr. Hepburn for entry into the rehab unit." Turning back to me, he added, "It should all take about two weeks if Dr. X accepts you. But I don't think there'll be a problem. I certainly would, if I were him." I wasn't sure what he meant by that remark, so I decided to give it the best possible interpretation, namely, that I was an outstanding patient with every chance of making a complete recovery.

I was conscious that it was through acquiring a positive mental framework that the rehab process was most likely to be effective. Did it come naturally? No the pattern that I had learned in childhood was that there was always a higher hilltop to aim for. So achievements were no more than a stepping stone to the next stone. (I know it's fashionable to blame parents or teachers for distorted learning, but I am not making anyone else to blame. I did the flawed learning, and now it was me who was doing the re-learning).

The rehab unit and the consultant that had been mentioned were the very ones that Allan had recommended. So, at this stage, there was definitely the feeling of a fair wind blowing in my sails.

There was no more bullying in the final two weeks. Apparently, one of the most influential charge nurses had called off the persecution on the grounds that I had been showing the shoots of recovery and wasn't just the waste of space I had appeared in the first few weeks of my illness. To my delight, this appeal had been accepted and my persecutors backed off completely.

On the day that the new consultant arrived to conduct my assessment I greeted him with the whole "excited dog" routine. Here was the man who had it in his power to take me out of this hospital where I had experienced such horrors, over such a long time. Even though the torture sessions had ceased over the last two weeks it was still my intention to get as far from these people as possible. They had demonstrated their potential and I was not going to hang around to let it happen again.

Throughout the consultant's assessment I was as compliant as possible, and as deferential as it was in my make-up to be. I did the equivalent of flexing my biceps at him. This was one gig I didn't want to miss so I pulled out all the stops. And, sure enough, he said at the end of his assessment that he would like to offer me a place in his rehab unit.

Cue another round of the "excited dog" routine. Then he added that it would be another two weeks before he had a spare bed. I wondered slightly at his ability to predict future bed availability with such precision. But a two-week wait, especially with the newly created entente-cordial, was no major problem. In fact, I'd even go so far as to say that I was beginning to quite like it there, which was as it should have been right from the start.

The answer to the question as to *why* I made the journey back from yogi to businessman is more difficult to answer, especially given my historical ambivalence to the world of business! I suppose it was similar to New Labour's belief (probably now their former belief,) that it was possible to sit down with the business fraternity, and discuss with them the common interest. We have all seen how that project ended up, and we have seen too, how an unfettered business sector can act with crass stupidity when the profit motive runs amok. In the light of what has transpired, I like to think that I would be working to channel businesses down a more constructive path, and not just taking the Queen's shilling. But, the need to earn a crust might have won out again!

When the day of departure actually arrived, it began with the arrival of some ambulance men to take me on my travels, and all my worldly belongings came with me, contained in two plastic bags. It was interesting because there were things in my cupboards that I hadn't seen since my very early days in hospital, things that looked very different now. To my complete surprise, I burst out into tears at the prospect of going out into the world again in such a weakened state. In this hospital, I was leaving behind all the people who had catered for my most basic needs and I hadn't yet met the people that were taking

their place. And so, the prospect of leaving this hospital suddenly seemed to create a big black hole for me to fill as soon as possible. I know it was a situation of my own making, but staying with the devil that I knew, suddenly appeared a more attractive option. It certainly seemed like I was taking this enormous leap into the darkness.

As I made my way down to the ambulance an elderly nurse came to the front and held my hand with great compassion and love in her eyes.

She was new to me, with an affection that seemed to signal that we had previously had some kind of relationship. I guessed that it must have been in the early phase of my illness, a phase when I really wasn't much aware. And with that, I was wheeled into the ambulance, still bawling. The ambulance men threatened to drop me off at the women's ward if I didn't stop bawling. That prospect seemed to have the desired effect, because I quickly calmed down. A new adventure was about to unfold and as my mind turned to that, I tried, but failed, to paint a picture of what that would look like.

Chapter 5 Rehabilitation

It was with anther metallic ping, and the whoosh of an opening lift door, that we finally arrived at the ward that was to be my home for the next year an a half. I was put directly in front of the nurses' station, which was perhaps three or four yards away. The nurses here all wore green tunics, with blue trousers, which contrasted sharply with the white tunics with which I had grown familiar over the last three months. So, right from the off, it seemed to me that they were just "pretend" nurses.

I was surprised also at just how vulnerable I felt being amongst strangers, and this time, in the bay of a ward, rather than in a private room. Social skills would be needed here, and yet I realised that my emotional lability could kick off at any second, and at the most inappropriate moments. This meant that socialising would be a tricky process, especially laughing at someone else's misfortune.

I must have been on some fairly strong medication when I arrived because I was only getting vague impressions of people, rather than sharp images. It all felt a bit surreal. A bit "Alice in Wonderlandish!" It didn't take me long to establish that the man in the next bed was allowed to go to the shops, without supervision. So there was something tangible to aim for. And, after six months, he was looking forward to resuming a "normal" life. This seemed to be a good template for my own recovery, only I hoped it would be a bit sooner!

On the first day, the ward doctor ran through my current meds before making a few changes. It was evident that there were some "professional differences" between the two hospitals, because some of the drugs on my current list seemed to evoke genuine surprise! Whatever, my drugs never caused me any more problems during my stay at that hospital.

I was asked, by various therapists, what my target was. In my job, I'd helped many companies to define their objectives. So, this was familiar territory for me. One thing I had noticed was how companies tended to play it safe, by designing targets that remained easily "attainable," and well within their comfort zones. Exceptional companies, on the other hand, deliberately set targets that involve a stretch. The important thing that came out of this, for me, was not to base the reward structure on the achievement of targets. In my experience, this encourages "secure" thinking, whereby managers set targets that they could be pretty assured of attaining. "Realistically" some of the great David and Goliath events in history shouldn't have happened. It was only by not thinking "realistically", but by dreaming unrealistically of "possibilities," that Davids, through the centuries, have been able to pull off surprise victories.

So, when it was necessary for me to specify objectives for my time spent in rehabilitation, I deliberately set "aspirational" objectives. The truth was, I had no idea how this was going to pan out, but I knew, from my experience in business, that my expectations would play a part in determining my actual performance. With hindsight, this decision might have been responsible for my lengthy stay in that hospital. I don't know for sure, but comments made during my stay there, lead me to conclude that the therapists wanted to see me "get real" with my expectations. For my part, I had no firm evidence on which to base any expectations. And, in its absence, it seemed wise to think big about resuming my travels down the highway.

One of the first nurses I connected with was a man in his early thirties. He took me under his wing, and was looking out for me throughout my stay. His attention to detail and common-sense approach was way beyond anything I'd experienced before in the NHS. And, more than that, there was his willingness to go the extra mile to make sure I was comfortable and safe. He single-handedly restored my faith in the NHS.

It was only after a year or so that it dawned on me that he was gay, and quite proud of it. Now I can be as homophobic as the next Scots man. Well, maybe not quite! I attempted to not make it a factor in my work.

Many of the most "damaged" people that I came across in my work were members of the gay community, who often had very low self-esteem generally after, in many cases, years of being persecuted and put down. (I've also met many gays who don't fall into this category, so this is not just another stereotype!) "Euan," as I'll call him, allowed me to see that gender preference is not really an issue when it comes down to the quality of the care provision.

Being only yards from the nurses' station and the seat of the ward secretary, I was able to hear a lot of confidential information that would otherwise have passed me by. For some reason, it did not occur to me that, just because I could overhear telephone conversations, that did not mean I had to listen in! To my amazement, the staff on nightshifts talked at normal volume all night long. And I just lay there, following the conversations, because I could. There was even a night when an African relief nurse spent the entire night giving out Swahili lessons. Next morning I may have been tired, but my Swahili grammar was pretty impressive!

The man opposite complained about the noise at night, and the night staff amazed me by removing themselves from the ward and sitting instead in a small room adjacent to the ward. I was so impressed by their responsiveness that I followed his example, a couple of weeks later, and following his discharge. I expected to elicit a similar, effortless response.

What I had not factored into the equation was that he held rank in the NHS family. He was a hospital consultant. His request had been accepted out of respect for his status in the family, whereas mine fell on deaf ears, with nobody changing their routine one iota. During his stay though, I watched the consultant metamorphise from a bed-ridden invalid into a determined speed walker, up and down the ward. I watched carefully all the different stages that he passed through, and worked out how I could shave time off each, so as to be back on my feet and out of here, as soon as possible.

The ward was comprised almost totally from wood, giving it the feel of a great big ship. Indeed, one of the first weird experiences that I had in this ward of brain-injured patients, was a young lad with short-term memory loss stemming from a bout of meningitis. He would make his way to the public telephone approximately once every hour, and would virtually repeat the same conversation, oblivious to the fact that he'd had that very conversation an hour previously. He would always lead off with the statement, namely that he had somehow got on a big boat! You can see that bound in with the tragedy there was also a comical dimension to this incident, for the first few hours at least!

At breakfast the next morning a man turned to me, a propos nothing, and said "I'm a spy, a secret agent. What do you do? " It was precisely situations like this that were guaranteed to trigger my lability, and the poor man was met by an outburst of hilarity that probably left him thinking that I was the one with the problem. And to some extent he was right. Because, during my stay on that ward I had no difficulty in seeing the behavioural flaws of those around me, but had little insight into why I was there. My guess is it was pretty much the same for everyone in there; the ability to recognise unusual traits in others, with a simultaneous inability to recognise what is abnormal in one's own behaviour.

This was perhaps best illustrated when a young "hooligan" joined the ward. He had been injured when some young boy, whom he had "given a good kicking to" a few weeks previously, decided to return the treatment, and in doing so, had inflicted a brain injury. He screamed abuse at the staff, and churned out some really vicious racism towards some of the black and Chinese staff. And he made it generally known that he wanted back out as soon as possible "to sort the boy out." So bad did it get, that I made my way up to his bedside in an electric chair to remonstrate with him. In my mind's eye, I was confronting him with a reasonable amount of authority. But with the benefit of hindsight, a non-speaking, partially paralysed man, in an electric wheelchair, was probably not the most threatening thing he had come across! It was no wonder that, among other more colourful words, he referred to me as a "mad cripple."

Interestingly, he told me a few weeks later, when his behaviour had modified, that "Everybody knew you were the coolest dude on the ward," and told me I had been the only person in the hospital to stand up to his outbursts!

Eventually, I insisted on being moved to a quieter spot, further from the nurses' station, and deeper in the bay. But then, when it was clear that I no longer required close supervision, I was moved all the way down to the other end of the ward, some one hundred and fifty yards from where I had started. At one level, I was proud of my new senior-ity but, on another, I felt distant from the hub of the action. My head was against the thin partition wall that screened off the TV area. It was something of a shock to be woken, in the middle of the night, and to hear the sound of the TV with flashes of light projected on the ceiling from the moving TV screen, as off-duty members of the night staff took in the news! Surely, this would not happen in a hospital, with brain damaged patients?I assumed this must be an aberration, and something that would not be repeated again, but it continued for several nights in a row.

In frustration, I eventually raised it with the charge nurse, who I ful-ly expected to be outraged by what was happening on her ward. And, she did appear to be incredulous about the scenario. But when I wait-ed for something dramatic to happen, as a consequence of my com-plaint, I got a real lesson in how ranks close in the NHS. Instead of leaving the TV alone, the staff now came to my curtained cubicle to check that I was asleep, before switching the TV on! And how do I know this? Because, despite appearances, I wasn't! It was apparent that my complaint had been discussed, but the outcome had not been as I expected. Was this merely the carping of a sick old man, or was it a sane response to an absurd situation? I'm not sure any more! One thing I am sure of is how the NHS family club together to get through crises, and to remain resilient in the face of outside threat. This is both its great strength, and its great weakness, in terms of its capacity to embrace change.

I finally came to terms with my "illusions" one day as I was trying to give a full account to a visitor, of all that I had been through in my previous hospital. I could see the look of incredulity cross his face, and his expression switched over to a sympathetic smile.

I was being pitied, and even as the words emerged from my lips I suddenly got that I had been nursing paranoid delusions for the last year! I almost simultaneously wondered why this had not occurred to me earlier, and how on earth they had got in there in the first place! It was definitely not in my nature to accommodate paranoid delusions, let alone, to be so utterly convinced by them. Now, at last, I could return to my former belief that the world was a benevolent place, with lots of agencies working together to improve things.

One other area where I got caught up in ward politics concerned the ward's attitude to children. The visiting children would clatter, as they ran down the length of the floor, shrieking at the top of their voices. And mothers would off-load their children in the TV area, and the newly arrived children would immediately change the station, oblivious to anyone else's preference. At the risk of sounding like a grumpy old man, I raised these issues with the charge nurse, whose reaction was that it was good for families to be able to meet up in the hospital!

Now I know this is true, for as a young child I used to make frequent trips to hospital to visit my own father. It seems to offer benefit to both patient and child. So, I would not want to jeopardise that. But, when I think back to my own childhood, there is no way that I would have expected hospital life to revolve around me. It's true that "times, they are a changin". I suppose that I am just questioning the wisdom of our institutions giving primacy to children, at all times. I have lived in America, and have seen the future, with doting grandparents, passively following the lead of a precocious child. It's not a pretty sight!

Being introduced to my new physio was never going to be easy, given the strength of my bonding with the physios in my previous hospital. And to begin with, there was very little chemistry between us. But by the time her placement on the ward was over, she had become like my big sister. She had that gift, which I have seen a few times, of making the client feel that there is no other more important patient in the hospital. And, she was willing to step outside her narrow professional remit, in order to facilitate other areas of my life in the hospital.

One unexpected development at around this time was that, contrary to my belief about putting in the necessary hours in the gym, as soon as my physio went off to attend to something else, my own exercise ground to a halt, irrespective of the task I had been set. To all intents and purposes, it seemed that I had turned into a shirker virtually overnight. This was not my normal pattern, and seemed to point to a worrying moral decline. I don't mind admitting that I was nervous about it.. I had never been a naturally gifted athlete, and had relied on my capacity for hard slog, not that it made much difference at 52 years of age!

So concerned was I about this development that I raised it with my physio. She did not look concerned about it and went ahead and explained that damage had been done to that part of my brain that memorised repetitive exercise. This meant that as soon as my conscious mind moved on to something else, my exercise activity came to an abrupt halt because there was nothing left to drive it.

This sounded suspiciously like one of the lame excuses that had been laid at my doorstep during my old days as a sports coach. So I decided to use will power to keep on track with my exercise regime, but to no avail. No matter how many times I set out, with bold intent, it became obvious that the end result was the same. As soon as my attention switched to something else, any exercise activity ground to a halt. What I learned was that exercise had to become a closely supervised activity or it didn't get done at all, no matter how noble my initial intention. This was a major blow to my ego and it caused me to update my sense of "who I had become."

My experience of Occupational Therapy was less good. For a start there was her job title. Now I didn't know what an "Occupational Therapist" was, but it sounded like a Government initiative to get me back to work, which didn't endear me to her! Then there were a series of strange rendezvous, called things like "dressing practice" and "breakfast practice," when I would sit passively and watch her doing the practice. It all seemed a bit weird. For "shower practice" I just sat on my shower chair and got showered as usual. Perhaps I was missing something.

Speech and Language therapy was a pleasant experience, but it has not achieved much improvement in my speech and language. At least it gave me the opportunity to address the speech difficulties arising from my constant drooling, and allowed me to make some painfully slow progress with my swallowing. By now, I had fully accepted the evidence that I could no longer swallow. What I could do though was to take on board the instructions that were being given and progress through the various stages towards normality. And after three more months, and swallowing X-rays being taken, I finally got there! It was with great pride that I completed my first hospital menu, and then joined the "big boys" in the canteen area for my very first meal in six months.

One exciting development during my time in this hospital was the introduction of a Lightwriter, a small computerised machine into which text could be typed, and then those words could be spoken out loud or scrolled for another to read. Although this was only useful for conveying fairly crude messages, without the subtleties of normal communication, let alone the skilled communication that had been the basis of my working life, it was still a major step forward as a way of getting my basic needs met. The downside was that people were free to read my words and then project any meaning they liked onto them. In this way, people projected whatever personality suited their interpretation of my words, which led to some odd scenarios! Also, I would answer whatever question I was asked, and often the question I was asked contained some false presuppositions. In this way, I would see communication gaps grow wider, and sometimes it was not possible to recover these, often leading to accusations of lying or deliberately misleading.

The consultant would tour the ward every week. He seldom examined patients so it was unclear how he was able to monitor progress. I think he must have placed great faith on the "intelligence" he gathered from his team of therapists. One day, I summoned up the courage to ask him the question I had been wrestling with for several months now. It was quite scary to put it out there, because, to some extent, I was losing control of the agenda. But, I had metaphorically kicking my heels in this ward for about a year, and I was getting frustrated! Certain that he would know the answer from his many years' experience

in this field I asked, "How much longer till I can expect a favourable wind to blow in my direction?" To my surprise, he burst out laughing and replied, "Oh, you want me to be a philosopher now!" He didn't, as I had expected, answer X months. But I was mystified by his reply, and for the first time in about fourteen months it occurred to me that perhaps there was no recovery to expect! Maybe this was just how it was going to be from now on.

You would have thought that this scenario would have crossed my mind a bit sooner, but it hadn't. And, for the very first time, I began to contemplate life as a disabled person, a group that I wasn't familiar with, and of whom, I had no direct experience. There was worse, it was about this time that my "On/off" relationship with physio finally came to an abrupt halt. When we were issued with our therapy timetable for the week ahead there was no mention of physio. This initially didn't concern me. I assumed there had been a clerical error, which would be rectified in minutes if I spoke to my "mates" in the gym. But on arriving nonchalantly at the gym I was told there would be no more physio, because my name had been put on a discharge list. Now I knew, from long experience, that this was not true. If anything, the physio effort would intensify prior to someone's discharge. The very sad conclusion was that the physios had made decisions about where to allocate their scarce resources. And I was no longer a priority! I had been dumped by the physios, without an honest explanation. With a painful thud, it dawned on me this was the end of the road! I wasn't deemed worthy of any more effort!

As you can imagine, this put a severe dent in my plans to rise Phoenix-like from the ashes! I searched around for an alternative way to interpret this development, but to no avail. The immensity of this situation finally got through to me. Although, on the surface, I carried on as usual, deep down I was hurting from this revelation.

It was about this time that I overheard the "foreign agent" say to one of his friends "Oh, it's not so bad in here, there's always somebody worse off than yourself!" It was a sentiment that I heartily agreed with, but the subsequent flash of his eyes in my direction was not expected. I had always assumed that his confusion about his identity and various other assorted wounds made him much worse off than me. His comment made me re-evaluate my situation. I had assumed that, because I was more or less the same person inside (minus sat nav) I had emerged on the other side fairly unscathed. Now that I had been abandoned by physiotherapy, and seemed destined for a life among the severely disabled, the situation was suddenly looking less appealing.

You may feel that this outcome was fairly predictable at a much earlier stage in the development of this story, but I had dared to dream of an almost total recovery, and it was a complete shock to me that now that dream was being snatched away.

But, what surprised me most was that there was no attempt to manage this development! It was as though the circus had just packed up and left town! The hospital did not cover itself with glory at these times.
When eventually I did get discharged, there was no discharge meeting to plan for a smooth transition into the community (despite me having requested one) and there were no meds or prescriptions to take home with me. It felt like a rather sordid end to an eighteen-month episode.

Another issue that interested me was just whom exactly I was emerging as, after this long ordeal? I had become a sort of "curmudgeon." I had checked several times that this curmudgeon was a congruent expression of my "true self" and each time I was satisfied that it was, even if it was at odds with the self that had set out on this adventure. My guess was that the difference was largely down to the missing sat-nav.

One other snatched conversation I overheard in the dining room involved an old age pensioner who was explaining, in incredulous tones, that he had been told that he would be staying in hospital for six nights!

There was a curious sense that people like him were just brain-injury "tourists" in a land inhabited by "long-distance travellers" like me.

Another incident involved a man we'll call Jack. Jack was a wheelchair user whose spine over the years had (apparently) become severely curved. This severely hampered his dexterity and every so often he would explode with a tirade of frustrated self-abuse.

I learned two things from observing Jack. The first, was to take postural advice seriously, even when there was little chance of any significant short term gains. And the second one, was to recognise that there might be times, in this strange half-life they called disability, when circumstances would prove frustrating. But I vowed never to turn in on myself with such self-hatred. A modicum of compassion for the self would be needed to get me through these choppy waters! So if "Jack" is reading this, as he was quite prone to, he should be aware that his misfortune was not completely in vain.

For the first year and a half, I took no interest in watching television. But when I did begin to watch it, it was intriguing to see presenters and their guests nearly two years down the line. I noticed subtle style changes in a way that you don't when you're absorbed in the constant evolution of trends. And faces had changed shape, reflecting weight loss and gain, and the affects also of ageing.

Soap storylines also had moved forward, with new characters added, and some missing. What was clear was that improbable character transitions had occurred, transitions that would probably have occurred gradually, over months, and been shown to have appeared as credible.

There were a whole new generation of adverts too. Though this too would probably have gone unnoticed in the context of the gradual evolution of the genre.

During my long wait on the ward, I also had the time to get some medical answers. Answers to questions like, "What exactly is a stroke?" Or, "Will my double vision resolve itself, in time?"

The answer to the first question was that a brain stem stroke was either a bleed or a clot in the back of the brain. In my case it had been a clot and they had identified a gene that predisposed my blood towards clotting. The resultant damage had been largely to the motor skills.

The answer to the second question was a bit vaguer leading me to conclude that things were a bit up in the air.

It annoyed me slightly that the medical staff were never as frank with me as they were with Pam. I had to glean information second-hand from Pam, which only added to the likelihood of distortions being introduced! But, above all, it struck me as a rather puerile way to conduct affairs. Was I regarded as incapable of sound judgement? As far as eyesight was concerned, I was eventually given the assurance that there was likely to be continued improvement in my double vision, though not probably 100%. And in addition, my brain was likely to adjust to the new situation by bringing the two images together to form a single image, for all practical purposes.

And so it turned out to be, although initially when I watched television there were two sets to choose from, about six feet apart. My confused eyes darted from one image to another.

One particularly poignant episode involved our cat, Ella. I had previously half-joked about its "top cat" status in our domestic hierarchy. It even routinely made a beeline for occupancy of my chair. Over the years there had been a constant battle between the two of us as to whose chair it was. It had always really been the apple of my wife's eye and she would sit with it beside her, purring noisily as my wife stroked it continuously.

Now clearly, that domestic bliss had been interrupted. My wife's world was currently organised around me, and had been for the last year and a half. Something would have had to lose out in order to accommodate this readjustment of our domestic priorities. It was obvious that in our case, it would have been Ella's domestic bliss. And sure enough, after a period of increased "pickiness" about food, it came as no great surprise to hear that Ella had gone to the great pet heaven in the sky, no doubt to a chair that was indisputably hers. I felt genuinely sorry that I had inadvertently cast a shadow over the last part of her life, and was, once more, amazed at my wife's apparent resilience, in the face of what, for her, must have been a very difficult time.

Chapter 6   The Unholy Trinity

As a result of some detective work by my hospital social worker, and some insider knowledge that my wife had gleaned from a social worker friend, (thanks K) I had been steered in the direction of "independent living" which didn't mean much to me from a hospital bed.
For my part, I just wanted to be released from, what had become, my prison.

As I mentioned at the beginning of this story, I am a fairly private person, so twenty-one months of life in the hospital system had left me quite shell-shocked and exhausted. Throughout this time I had become "public property" to be stripped and washed at will. Although I had not realised it at the time, this had been a lengthy ordeal for me.

I don't think I realised during my time in hospital just how difficult it had all been for me, to be "trapped" in that system for so long. While in hospital, I had no clear reference as to how I would live after my "release."

Quite frankly, when some officials took the decision that my family home was not suitable accommodation for me, I thought it was just officials being officious, and that a way would be found eventually to make it manageable for me to live there. So, when new accommodation was finally discussed, there was only a part of me involved because the rest of me was primed like a homing pigeon, to head back to where I had come from. But, sure enough, when the day of leaving hospital finally arrived, I was sent off in a new direction, and with a new set of keys.

Initially, I sat in the garden just letting the past twenty one months blow out of my hair. The process of adjustment had started, but was now about to be interrupted by another unexpected development. On the third morning of my discharge from hospital I awoke with a stinging sensation in my groin. There was no sense among my support workers of it being a major problem, but we decided to call in the doctor in any case for a proper examination. It took about four hours for the doctor to arrive so I just stayed in bed to allow for a thorough examination to take place.

It was with real sadness that I heard the news that the doctor thought it best that I get it checked over by the hospital. Frankly, I thought he was being overly cautious in sending me to a hospital. I thought his decision was influenced by my recent health scare. However, if this was another hoop that I needed to jump through in order to get a quiet life, then so be it.

It took a further five hours for the ambulance to arrive and then the trip to the hospital began. This time it was a third hospital, one that I had never been in before. With all my hospital experience behind me, I was not too concerned about what lay in front of me.

I don't remember much about my arrival in hospital, which may have been down to the fact that I was unconscious. I'm not sure. Anyway the story goes that they ran with me on a trolley down to the theatre, where I had an emergency operation for gangrene.

During my recovery I was conscious of a large pool of blood gathering near my wound. For some reason, I felt content to watch this pool grow bigger and didn't feel the need to intervene. It was only when I began to shiver at the sharp drop in my body temperature that the nurses in intensive care latched on to the fact that something was amiss. I remember being colder than at any time in my life. It was as though my body had been taken out of a fridge. Like a cold chicken! The nurses, probably noticing my growing dis-ease, tried to reassure me by saying "Don't worry dear, you'll feel better when we get some blood into you!"

I woke up the next morning and was very happy to note that things were indeed back to normal. My medical notes refer to a resuscitation involving five pints of blood. As a medically uneducated layman, I'm not sure whether this means that I had stopped living for a while. My notes also refer to both my lungs collapsing and acute renal failure, but I'm not sure where in my time-line these occurred.

My circulation even these days is not good, so that when I begin to get cold, I vividly remember those few minutes! I should add that the quality of the nursing, both here and in the High Dependency Unit, which was to follow, was superb, and light-years away from life on the general wards. They worked through their tasks with real professionalism and with a great deal of intelligent awareness. This was what I had expected to encounter in the acute stroke ward!

Having been unconscious during most of the gangrene business, I thought that that this operation was still pending. So, when a consultant arrived to speak with me I naturally assumed that he had come to discuss, what I thought was, my forthcoming gangrene operation. It was something of a surprise when he talked about three separate treatments that he was proposing. Firstly, for recovery from my gangrene op. But then secondly, for a case of pneumonia that had been diagnosed, together with a dose of MRSA that they had come across.

My elation at having the worst of the gangrene business behind me was now overtaken by the realisation that I still had two other tests to come. To win out on all three fronts was going to be a big challenge, and I was still weak from the first. ! Things were not looking too bright. Never mind, the consultant looked like a confident opening batsman with a certain aura of success. I judged that I was in good hands and gave my blessing for the battle to start, even if deep inside I still thought it might be one of the last things I would do!

I don't remember much about the operations though I was pleasantly surprised to see one of my favourite nurses from my previous hospital in attendance throughout. During one of the operations I was aware of large globules of light being moved around. I remember being surprised that the NHS was now working in this way.

There is surprisingly little recollection of this time. What I do remember is wakening up after it was all over to find the little black mice running all across my eyeballs once again. I assumed I must have had another stroke as it was so reminiscent of the last time, and I had learned that it is only when you awaken after a stroke that you fully grasp that you've had one. Under the circumstances, it seemed most likely that it was a stroke from which I was awakening. My recollection of the illnesses that had brought me into hospital originally was absent, and it was all very depressing for those first few moments.

The bags of liquid feed were back, this time passing down a grey tube which ran directly down into my stomach, rather than via the little PEG feeding tube which had started to heal over. In addition, I was too weak to press down on my lightwriter keys (or, for that matter, my call button) so I was forced to fall back on my alphabet board with no greater success, this time round! All together, it looked like I was back where I had been two years prior and I could sense a big black cloud of depression headed my way. I didn't have much experience of successfully fighting back after such an onslaught of bad breaks, but I knew that staying focussed was going to be key to emerging successfully from this little lot. So, I decided just to overcome whatever obstacles were put in my way.

One of the treatments, for pneumonia I think, involved wearing a mask, not unlike a welding mask, for three days and nights.

Now, what made this mask unique was that there were continuous projections on the inside of the mask, in beautiful colour, of First World War scenes, together with a continuous auditory roll call of the allied dead. These continued, day and night, for the three days.

Added to which, it was one of the hottest summers on record and the hospital was coping particularly badly with the heat, so putting my head in the mask was like putting my head in a sauna. My consultants made pretty clear that this was my last hope of survival and that they were sceptical of my ability to stay in the mask for three days (and they didn't even know about the in-mask entertainment!) This was definitely the hardest thing I had been asked to do in the last two years.

As when I was going for my PEG operation, it felt that closed eyes and gritted teeth would be required to take me through to the finishing line. That, and a great store of focus and single-mindedness, which fortunately I had learned in the mountains of India.
The one comforting thought was that, with each passing moment, I was closer to the finishing line. And I was actively counting down the seconds!

It was with tremendous relief that I finally staggered across that finishing line, taking everyone by surprise! It was the most difficult ordeal of my life to date, and not one that I look forward to repeating. There followed two more weeks of using a nebuliser, twice a day, for ten minutes each time. These were little masks into which oxygen was fed continuously. Although the circumstances were less severe than the last mask, I still hated these sessions. I would count down the minutes and the seconds left till it was all over!

Another delight was from the use of cough stimulators! My recollection, which could be a distortion of the truth, is that long pieces of a wire contraption were fed down my throat and then "triggered" in some way to stimulate a cough reflex. Although this wasn't a pleasant experience, it was not as arduous as wearing the facemask.

I remember it was not long after I made it back onto the general ward that I was teamed up with a male African nursing assistant. He put the radio on and I recollect that there was one of these radio phone-in quizzes broadcast, as he was working with me. The question was along the lines of, "What is the name of the pub in the TV programme 'Coronation Street?' Is it a) The Rover's Return, b) The Woolpack, or c) The Queen Vic? Something that virtually any T.V. watcher in Britain would know.

I remembered the look of excitement that came with the realisation that he knew the answer.

I don't know how he perceived the situation, but it struck me that here was a man who had made it to the rich man's table, but to stay at that table with any measure of comfort would require the intervention of Lady Luck. Accordingly, he took out his mobile phone and called in the answer. I had often wondered towards what sort of market these "quizzes" were targeted at. And now, I had the answer, at least to my own satisfaction!

One other male nurse I remember from around this time was an American, who, uniquely, seemed to understand bed craft. He opened my eyes to a whole new world of bed manoeuvrability. And, like all the other stars I had met along the way, he would "go that extra mile," dropping in before his shift began, and after his shift had ended.

The nursing staff were very encouraging about my little "setback" and suggested that it might not take as long as I thought to get back to the level that I had been at prior to my most recent episode. And, much to my surprise, that's how it turned out. I resumed eating solids within a couple of weeks, although the dietician made it clear that I wouldn't be leaving until I had put on some weight. In response, I started to devour four or five yoghurts, or high protein drinks, with every meal. I had clocked up a total of nearly two years in hospital wards! I didn't want to spend a day longer than was necessary.

My electric wheelchair was brought to the hospital. It was curious. Like looking at what had been my favourite walking stick from a previous birth. On the one hand, it looked very familiar, and on the other, it didn't seem to be a part of my life any more. Maybe, it was like sifting through childhood toys.

What I didn't expect was that my accumulated tolerance of being able to remain seated on the chair for several hours would be completely wiped out. After about forty minutes in my chair the pressure became unbearable, as before. Unfortunately, I'd forgotten that all NHS staff disappear for a couple of hours each day. Very often it was like the Mary Celeste. Thousands of pounds worth of expensive equipment lying around, but no member of the nursing staff to be seen. There must be an NHS heaven somewhere, where the missing NHS staff meet up. Perhaps it's close to the place where all those single socks gather!

So, once again, it was proving hazardous to ask to be put in wheelchair in the fist place. Careful planning was necessary to make sure that not only was there sufficient staff to get me in the chair, but sufficient numbers to get me back out, if necessary.

One day, I was asked to make a "home visit" with a selected "gaggle" of professionals, so that they could "risk assess" my living environment. It was on the appointed day after completion of my safety audit that they suddenly announced that I could stay on, if I wanted. The thought had not crossed my mind. I had not said goodbye to anyone and had various plans outlined for the next few days. Nevertheless, it was an opportunity to escape from a hospital system that had had me in its grips now for about two years!

There was no real chance of me going back voluntarily, however abrupt the end had come. But it was not the ending I would have chosen. And this time, there was a (very good) crisis care team to iron out any teething problems in the first few days back.

This last episode had taken three months to unfold and I escaped from that hospital with a distinct feeling of having survived a very close thing.

If I hadn't felt very "lucky" when news of the unholy trinity first broke, I now felt like a lottery millionaire.

Chapter 7 Life on the Outside

Back in the land of the living, it was initially quite a shock to discover how much my status had changed. Before, there was the comfort from knowing that I was part of the "engine of the economy." In fact there was the quiet satisfaction that came from the knowledge that I was helping to make that engine "purr" more every day. Contrast that then with the realisation that from now on I was likely to be a burden on the state!

I was genuinely moved by the fact that I belonged to a society that made reasonable provision for people like me, who had fallen off the edge of the world. There was a safety net in place, willingly supported financially by a society that deemed it politically appropriate for such a net to be in position, (written before Mr Cameron's "cost-cutting").

I don't mind admitting that I was touched by that! And more, I discovered that there was a vast army of helpers, trained and in position to do their bit. It was obviously organised like a big Mafia because bits of information were circulated around, unseen, triggering all sorts of professionals to emerge from out of the woodwork.

I know that there is constant competition for funding, and there is never enough money to buy other than the most primitive of equipment, but we can celebrate the fact that we belong to a society that at least makes a stab at caring for us!

It was really a case of start again, because any benefit gained in my previous short stay at home was now well and truly dissipated by my most recent bout of hospital-itis. The one positive I brought back with me was hope. A belief that what doesn't kill you makes you stronger. I felt like I had come out victorious from a fairly major scrap, and that maybe the wind was about to change direction for me! If there was going to be a time for recuperation and things getting back on course, then maybe it would be now?

In the meantime I had the opportunity to get acquainted with "life in the community," a term I had heard many times, but about which, I knew very little in practice. I quickly got that my constant stream of nurses had now been replaced by a constant stream of support workers. I had mixed feelings about that. There was something comforting about being so close to medical expertise and to be surrounded by clinical hygiene! On the other hand, I quite liked the informality of my new minders! And clinical hygiene had not saved me from MRSA!

My support team made it clear that there were some circumstances where, as far as they were concerned, it would be appropriate for them to provide support and other circumstances where it would not. It looked like there were some rules of support work that I would have to learn quickly! I suppose there was an element of frustration that I was being offered a generic model of support work, rather than one that was designed around my specific needs. What became apparent very early was that if I was going to get any of my needs met, then it would have to be through the effective use of my support workers. Welcome to the world of dependency!

It was a trait that I had previously shunned, but one which I'd have to learn to use skilfully, if I was to avoid a life of frustration. The charge of manipulation is often laid at the feet of the disabled, but it is often a case of doing what little you can to get a satisfactory outcome. If manipulation is the only way of achieving the task, then so be it! It would never be my preferred option, but as a last resort, in a tough situation?

I was coming from a corporate environment, inhabited by executives who had risen to the ranks of management by grasping that it was their responsibility, in whatever context, to "make things happen." But, it became clear that I was dealing with a very different animal now though, and it was down to me to do something different, in order to get results. In business, we talk a lot about preserving the balance between task and relationships so that things get done, but preferably in a way that preserves relationships. However, my support workers presented a very different profile. For they, typically, valued relationships much more than task completion. In some instances even, they would be prepared to entirely abandon the completion of a task, if they thought that something of even more importance was being comprised.

I want to emphasise that this in no way intended as a criticism of my carers, who thankfully possess a different value-set to the one I was more familiar with in the upper echelons of business management. Rather, it is an acknowledgement that, if I wanted to get things done, I would clearly have to do something different. To begin with, I noticed how tasks often faltered at the first hurdle. When I explored this, I discovered that my framing of the task was too vague for easy understanding, and that by breaking the overall task down into smaller "stepping stones" I made the chances of success much greater. But the other thing I noticed was how quickly and completely meaning became distorted as communication was passed on. Even when I asked that notes be taken, as reminders, the problem did not go away.

Eventually, I realised that the answer to this problem was to type out a message and to ask for it to be read out verbatim. Even then, there would be a significant change in the message as a result of different stresses and emphasis. But hey, that's as good as it gets, and I have learned not to be too attached to these things. Probably my wife is the only one who knows me well enough to know how I structure my sentences (and probably wishes she didn't most of the time!)

What does still bother me is that I have very little control over where things are stored when my back's turned! I have tried my best to create "homes" for different kinds of items, but we are still in a situation where I can buy something one day, only to have it "stored" away in the oddest of places next day. This state of permanent "disorganisation" is probably the hardest aspect of disabled life to accept; life in a continual state of flux. Again I want to emphasise that this is not criticism of my support team, who work very hard to make things as I want them (mostly!) Rather it is an acknowledgement that when the organisation of your life is in the hands of a large group of people, there's bound to be some degree of havoc! The way I cope with this permanent state of flux is to have as little attachment as possible to items in my flat, but I do continue to find this a difficult area, especially when some of my closest relatives interpret my efforts at detachment as careless indifference.

When things are your own you handle them with care, and use up as little as possible, to extend the item's useful life. But in the hands of paid employees, the rules of stewardship seem to change and it is painful to look on and see even new items being destroyed or needlessly exhausted!

One thing I became aware of quite quickly was that my support staff each excelled in different areas, and it was important to select the correct staff member for the task in hand. Or, failing this, to modify the task so that it fell within the range of competency of the staff member on duty. Initially I would ask the wrong staff member to look for a certain item in a drawer, only to get a cast iron assurance that, "the item wasn't there." When I asked the correct staff member to look for the same item next day it would mysteriously appear! This rule seemed to apply equally for cooking, cleaning, or computer problems. To some staff members, these would pose a problem, while for others, they were simple tasks.

The first few weeks in my flat were difficult. I likened it to having fallen into a bear trap. One minute, there I was, strolling nonchalantly along the path, and the next all hell breaks out, as I tumble, head first, into a hole that seemed destined to be my home for the rest of my life, which suddenly doesn't appear that much longer.

My entire relationship to this life and to this planet was suddenly being renegotiated, and the package on offer didn't seem all that attractive! But, above all, there was a recurring thought that I was meant to be going somewhere. That being isolated and trapped in this dark hole was not what I was meant to be doing with my life. It didn't tally with my understanding of "why I was here." This was a full-blown case of existential anxiety and would be accompanied by panic attacks during which I would feel certain that this was just another situation for which there must be a solution, if only I could find it! This would be accompanied by a quick search for all possible escape routes. And would end with bitter disappointment that all exits seemed to be barred! These panic attacks were almost invariably followed by a sleepless night, during which, I would walk round the perimeter, testing every meter in my mind.

One strange development around this time was an organised trip to a day centre. Now I had no idea what a "day centre" was, let alone what significance it might have for me, although it had probably been explained.

I agreed to go along out of curiosity. Turns out, it was a place where other disabled people congregated in a sort of adult "youth club." I was told that I met all the criteria to attend the day centre and that a letter offering me a place would probably follow in due course. I really still had no idea what a day centre would do for me, but was pleased to be in demand, nevertheless.

On the first morning I was due to attend, a municipal white bus came to meet me, its seats packed with other attendees. I suppose my first reaction was to want to sit up front, with the driver. The bus was full of people with some very special needs, and in this situation, I did not yet identify myself with them. The driver, on the other hand, I could identify with. He was operating out of a skill-set that I knew well, as was the bus care assistant.

As the bus meandered up to the day centre, it seemed strange to be sitting there, amongst them. We passed office blocks I had worked in during my career, and that world seemed a lot more "real" to me than the one I was currently sitting in. Even when we finally arrived at our destination, I still felt that some mistake had been made, that I didn't really belong in this subset of society. And when I looked out from the bus at the clients crossing the car park in order to enter the front door of the centre, it was like a scene from "Shaun of the Dead" as groups of people, with very different disabilities, dragged them-selves towards the door! This condition had clearly stolen a great deal from people.

Once again, there was the instinct to run. I knew that to go in meant me accepting, perhaps for the first time, that I now belonged in this strange community called "the disabled." For the first few weeks I even tried to prove to the staff that I was different from the rest, that I was really one of them in disguise, but, no matter how hard I tried, the attitude of the staff remained firmly that of carer/client. Eventually, over months and years, it began to sink in that, not only was this my new peer group, but even amongst that peer group, I was one of the most severely disabled.

The alertness of the staff there was like nothing I had experienced before. Whereas, in parts of the hospital, as I have mentioned, things appeared to go unnoticed, here needs seemed to be anticipated from just a change of expression on your face! Attentiveness and safety-consciousness appeared to be standardised across the staff and "visual-acuity" seemed to be present in bucket loads! The level of
It had been a circuitous route, and not the clean-cut ending I had

personal support and guidance that was provided, by specialist staff, was also superb. If I didn't get a lot out of the social side of the centre, I certainly got a great deal from being in regular contact with such a highly skilled group of people! If I could wish them anything it would be more happiness. I realise that their work is always surrounded by tragedy, and that must be very wearing, but such a dedicated group of people deserve to bring happiness into their lives.

The one activity I got heavily involved in was art therapy. I suppose it gave me an outlet to express some of the more complex ideas running through my head. I've attached some of the work that came out of this class as Appendix 2. Some of it relates to what has been discussed here, in this book.

But the most important and valuable development to come out of my time in the community was my rediscovery of the ability to meditate. Whether this was the rediscovery of a part of the brain that had just been lying dormant, or the creation of new neural pathways, the fact remained that I could once more escape the limitations of my half frozen body.

It was much as I had said to those prisoners in India all those years before. I was now in an ideal situation to meditate. To escape from the consciousness of my body, and fly far above this sordid little scenario. At last, I was free from my bear trap. I knew that if I thought hard enough I would find it. There is a solution for every problem, if only I can find it!

The first thing that I became aware of in meditation was how many knots had developed in the physical body, knots that presumably had been there for some time, but of which I had been totally unaware. As a friend put it, my "default" had been changed without my knowledge.

So, the second development in meditation was when these knots started to unwind, which would happen for no apparent reason and at no particular stage of the meditation.

A third stage was reached when I became aware of the incessant chatter inside my head. I don't know if this was a habit that I had developed during my lengthy stay in hospital, but it was a habit that I had emerged with, a habit which meant that even the most peaceful of scenarios was spoilt by incessant chatter.

Mostly, we think of ourselves as the "victims" of our thoughts. But, as I have already mentioned "victimhood" did not sit easily on my shoulders. I was reminded by the process of meditation that it is possible to become aware of this running commentary then roll it back, so that there is only silence between the ears. You could say it was a blessed relief after all these years!

But perhaps the most important dimension to all of this was the restoration of the faith that, inevitably, things would turn out well in the end, no matter how bleak they looked in the short term. Nobel prize-winner, Albert Schweitzer was famously asked what was the most significant question that we could ask? His reply was, "Whether the Universe was a benign place to be, or a hostile place to be?"

I had been reminded of this question during my darkest days in hospital, shortly after my stroke. At the time, the evidence seemed to point pretty conclusively to it being a hostile place. And this frame of reference had persisted to this day. Every minor infection was taken as evidence that the Grim Reaper was rattling my door, yet again!

The future was a dark place to be, with the awareness that, sooner or later, the Reaper would prevail. The game was loaded in his favour! This awareness rather took the shine off whatever time was left. (And, lest this is seen as total paranoia, six out of eight students in my day-centre art class had recently "passed on.")

It had been a circuitous route, and not the clean-cut ending I had hoped for. But I was reconnected with my coping mechanism, and so was able to face whatever life threw at me!

And perhaps most importantly of all, the future did not seem like the bleak place it once had.

Chapter 8 The Future

All Good.....................

A Most Curious Detour

Appendix 1

With some of the Ashram residents (author to left of tree).

The author in full flow, shortly before being handed note

That lecture in Lima, as photographed (poorly) by my gifted camera.

Meeting with Indian Prime Minister Desai on a previous trip (author centre back).

A Most Curious Detour

Appendix 2

These art works illustrate the change in my consciousness over five years.

The picture depicts the moment when the stroke occurred and my life radically changed direction

The conveyor belt of life, with its many distractions along the way.

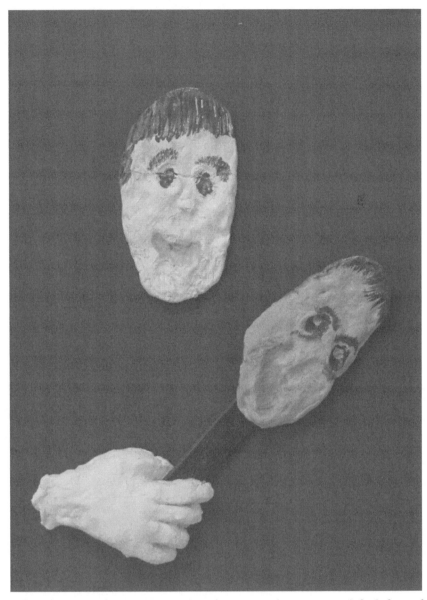

This sculpture depicts how I go to the mirror expecting to see my default face, of mild happiness and the sweet taste of success on my lips, only to find looking back at me a mask I barely recognise. In my previous life experience, I had learned the art of giving what the Indians call "Drishti" the art of communicating through the eyes alone. Now I see just pain and fear in those eyes, the eyes of the mask.

Out of Bounds - A reflection on the places I can no longer visit

Role reversal as the champion becomes the totally dependent

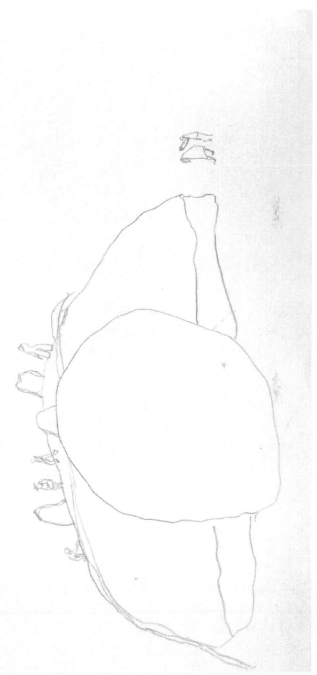

A favourite childhood image from Gulliver's Travels which encapsulates the experience of being worked on by carers

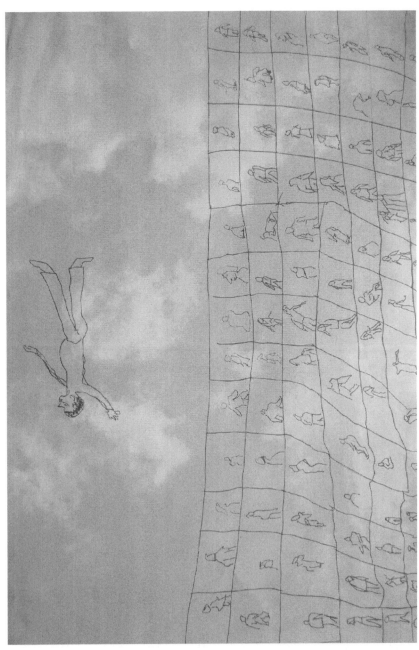

The realisation that, for my safety net to be in place, a high level of co-ordination and co-operation between different individuals is required

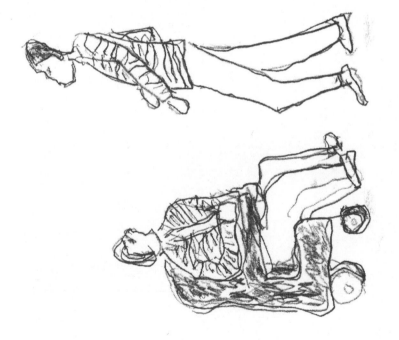

Walking nonchantly past myself, oblivious to wheelchair self, not through malice, but by focus being elsewhere.

This painting depicts my experience of being trapped in a cave, while observing the planet heading for its' destruction. It also shows my sense of frustration at not being out there making things happen.

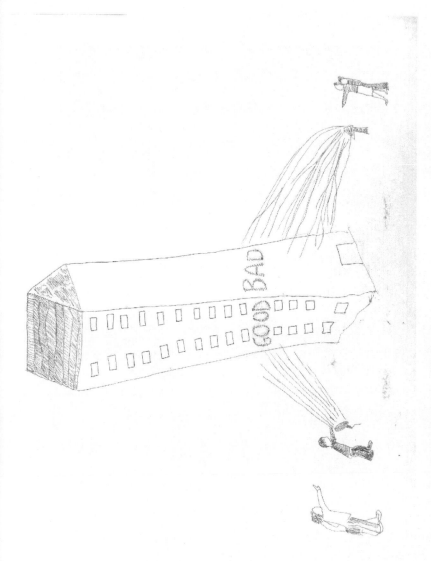

The building is busy just being a building while others project onto it what they see.

This work was inspired by the "love Boat'" idea that the party of life continues to sail, no matter who gets on or off

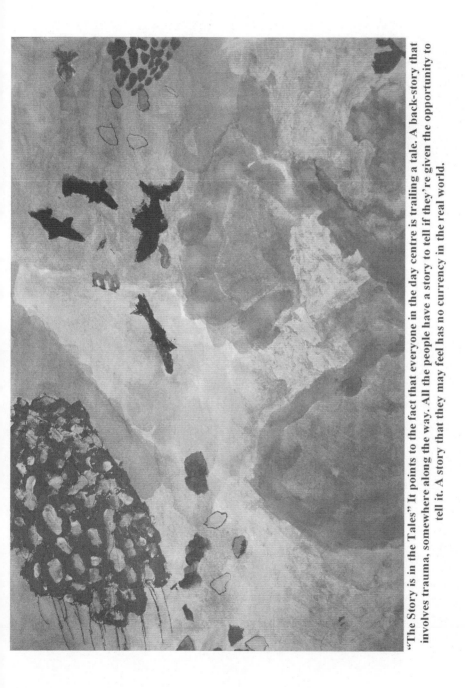

"The Story is in the Tales" It points to the fact that everyone in the day centre is trailing a tale. A back-story that involves trauma, somewhere along the way. All the people have a story to tell if they're given the opportunity to tell it. A story that they may feel has no currency in the real world.

It is not the hand you are dealt that defines you, it is what you do with the hand you are dealt

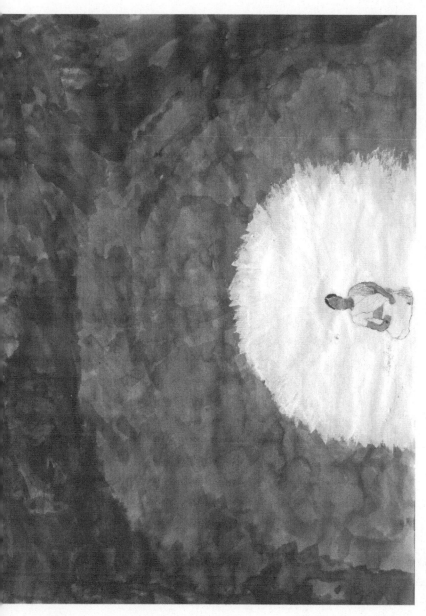

"Aura" – This marks the progression from the card player picture, the movement from words into silence

Watching the drama in the acute ward, with vague extras gathering in the wings.

A Most Curious Detour

Contact Details

For more information about Raja Yoga go to:
www.bkwsu.org/uk

To contact the author
go to: mostcuriousdetour@gmail.com

Back Cover

"Colour and Grey"

This picture represents a timeline in which a traumatic event instantaneously changed the quality of my experience from vibrant colour to shades of grey.

A Most Curious Detour

A Most Curious Detour

A Most Curious Detour

A Most Curious Detour

A Most Curious Detour